Woman's Day® PRIZEWINNING GRANNY SQUARES

Theresa Capuana,

Needlework and Creative Crafts Editor, *Woman's Day*®

Meredith® **Press**
New York

Dear Crocheter,

We're please to publish this collection of granny squares chosen as prize-winners by the editors of *Woman's Day* magazine.

Many of us who love to crochet learned at our grandmother's knee or from a close friend or relative. For this reason, special memories may often be bound up in the threads that we hold in our hands when we crochet. Granny squares, frequently our first attempt at crochet, suggest a link in the tradition of passing along needlework skills from one generation to the next.

Woman's Day Prizewinning Granny Squares has more than 40 original granny designs, including colorful florals, striking three-dimensionals, unique quilt-block patterns, and favorite traditional grannies with some new twists. Choose your favorite square then follow the clear, step-by-step instructions to make an afghan you'll prize, or let the squares inspire you to create any number of winning projects of your own design. You'll love working these beautiful squares every bit as much as the judges did selecting them.

Meredith® Press is proud of *Woman's Day Prizewinning Granny Squares*, as we are of all the high-quality craft books we publish. We hope you'll agree that we have succeeded in providing our readers with books containing a variety of projects for every skill level; accurate, easy-to-follow instructions; full-color photographs, and clear diagrams and patterns.

Best wishes for many happy hours spent crocheting.

Sincerely,

Barbara S. Machtiger
Barbara S. Machtiger
Editorial Project Manager
Meredith® Press

For Woman's Day®:

Editorial Project Manager: Geraldine Rhoads
Needlework and Creative Crafts Editor: Theresa Capuana
Project Editor/Writer: Roslyn Siegel
How-to Writer: Ellen Liberles
How-to Consultant: Ruth Jacksier
Illustrator: Roberta Frauwirth
Stylists: Karen Lidbeck, Richard Kollath,
   Woman's Day Needlework and Crafts Department
Administrative Assistant: Grace Westing
Photography: William Seitz, Julie Gang
Closeups: *Woman's Day* Studio

For Meredith® Press:

Director: Elizabeth P. Rice
Editorial Project Manager: Barbara Machtiger
Project Editor: Sydne Matus
Editorial Assistant: Valerie Martone
Production Manager: Bill Rose
Designer: Remo Cosentino/Bookgraphics

Copyright © 1990 by Diamandis Communications Inc. Projects copyright © 1988, 1989 by Diamandis Communications Inc. All rights reserved. All photographs in this book are the property of *Woman's Day* magazine. *Woman's Day*® is a registered trademark of Diamandis Communications Inc.

ISBN: 0-696-02343-1
Library of Congress Catalog Number: 89-063580
Printed in the United States of America
10 9 8 7 6 5 4 3 2 1

Contents

In the following list we have starred the projects according to their degree of difficulty. One star (*) designates an easy project, ** one that's fairly easy, *** a project of moderate difficulty, and **** one offering considerable challenge. Don't let the ratings daunt you; they are only estimates. Some experienced crocheters work entirely from pictures, and some beginners follow written instructions really well, so it is impossible to be accurate about the amount of skill a crocheter needs for each afghan. Remember, even the most challenging afghan may offer squares that can be used in smaller projects.

4

Introduction

Most women who learn to crochet sooner or later make granny squares. These small individual units have an enormous versatility, an energy all their own. By combining stitches to make one square and then carefully organizing the arrangement of the squares, it is possible to get an interplay of pattern and design that is exciting and highly original. To tap some of this originality among *Woman's Day* readers, and to encourage others to try out new ideas, the *Woman's Day* Granny Square Contest was launched. This book features the work of forty-one craftswomen whose outstanding and original designs were awarded prizes by *Woman's Day*'s panel of judges.

No one quite knows how and where the concept of crocheting "granny squares" originated. For certain, it is an ideal way to use leftover yarn. It is known that, as the name suggests, it is a skill passed down from mother to daughter. The first granny, whoever she was, must also have realized that the idea of creating individual units and then joining them to make an afghan, quilt, throw, vest, sweater, or cap had an enchanting simplicity about it. Like building blocks, or bricks, or even words in a sentence, these small, brightly colored units could be combined and transformed into something much more significant than themselves. They must have appealed to the first granny, as to generations of women following her, for their practicality, their portability, and their promise.

The women whose work is featured in this book have been drawn to granny squares for all these reasons and one or two of their own. Some have talked of the desire to do something with their hands in the evening while watching TV. Others have described the therapeutic value of crocheting: the regular, rhythmic dance of the hook and its calming effect. Some have crocheted granny squares to help earn a living; others to create a loving, unique gift for a sister's wedding, a daughter's room, a baby's birth. For some women crocheting has been a supplement to another craft, like weaving or painting; for others a welcome contrast to their careers.

It was exciting to discover how many different kinds of women are drawn to making granny squares. The women featured in this book come from twenty different states. There are young unmarried women, middle-aged mothers, and great-grandmothers. They live on farms, in small towns, and in big cities. They have careers in science, business, art, theater, and government. One is in the Marines.

Most of the women learned the basic crochet stitches from their mothers and grandmothers. Then they learned more intricate stitches and patterns from magazines and books such as this one. Most have passed on their skills to their own daughters and granddaughters.

It seems that the habit of using one's hands spills over into other hobbies and crafts. Women who make granny squares also seem to like other needlework. Many of the women featured here are proficient in knitting, quilting, embroidery, and needlepoint. Several are painters or weavers, the love of texture and color attracting them from one medium to another.

One of the special attractions of granny squares is their size and portability. One square takes only a few minutes to complete, requiring only a hook and a little bit of yarn, which will easily fit into an ordinary pocketbook. One of the women featured here completed an entire afghan riding to work on the bus. Another finished her quilt during theatrical rehearsals. Even ripping out is easy when you are working on a small unit. For the woman who is easily bored, small squares with the potential for variation offer a welcome change.

These prizewinning granny squares have been chosen for their originality, execution, and color. They have been inspired by mountains, wildflowers, and mulberries, executed in favorite colors, and designed with love. A number have been influenced by quilt or knitting designs. In arriving at their final patterns, the craftswomen experimented with different-shaped units. Many are not granny squares at all, but granny hexagons, rounds, hearts, or triangles. They utilize a number of different stitches and combine colors in subtle, and sometimes unexpected, ways. The finished squares are carefully arranged to create an overall pattern that often tricks the eye with optical illusions of shape and dimension.

The designs have been keyed for level of difficulty. Most fall in the middle range, en-couraging beginners to stretch their skills and allowing more accomplished crocheters to add new patterns to their repertoires. A few projects will provide delightful challenges for the experts. The projects took their designers anywhere from two weeks to a year to complete.

To make this book as convenient as possible to use, the patterns are arranged into four sections based on design motif: Traditional Patterns and Variations, Quilt Block Patterns, Dimensionals, and Florals. The design categories are broad, and not mutually exclusive. Many projects cross over into another category (for example, some Floral designs are also Traditional, some Dimensionals are Floral), so be sure to look through all the categories before you select your project.

Be excited by the patterns, colors, and textures within this book, but do not stop there. Let this book serve as a guide to the possibilities that you might create yourself using your imagination and your own favorite colors. Don't be afraid to mix textures—shiny rayon yarn with fluffy mohair or flat cotton. If one color doesn't work, save it for your next project and try another. Many of our contest winners made their afghans, throws, and lap robes with leftover yarn. Once you finish your squares, combine and recombine them until you have the arrangement you like. Or even use the squares in another project. This book features afghans, throws, and pillows, but there is no reason you cannot use your granny squares for vests, caps, or sweaters. Use this book as inspiration and enjoy expanding your own repertoire of stitches, patterns, and designs.

Traditional Patterns and Variations

The beauty of these afghans comes from using traditional granny units and stitches in unique and extraordinary ways. The colors, size, and placement of the squares, and the surrounding designs, create exciting one-of-a-kind originals.

Bordered Beauty

**The dramatic black-and-white border framing
the glowing colors of these traditional grannies
earned the afghan second prize.**

Becky Bohlinger
Pleasanton, California

Becky Bohlinger, the mother of two teenage children, spends most days working with youth and church groups, doing part-time computer work, and professional dressmaking. Never too tired to crochet, Becky says, "I love to work on a project in the evening, when the busy, hectic day has quieted down and I'm watching TV with the family. I'm so used to doing something that now it's hard for me to sit and watch TV empty-handed."

Her multicolored throw with its spectacular black-and-white border represents the solution to an artistic problem. She was given a bag of yarn with some squares already completed by her grandmother. She had no idea what her grandmother had in mind for the squares, but she did want to preserve the work in some way. Becky's answer was to make a patchwork afghan. She finished the squares with random colors and sewed them together to make a rectangle. Then she bordered the whole with black and white. This, she says, is "truly my granny-square afghan."

SIZE

About 44" × 56"

MATERIALS

Yarn: Knitting worsted, 22 oz. black (color A), 16 oz. white (B), 3½ oz. light green (C), 2 oz. rainbow variegated (D), 7 oz. assorted bright colors.

Crochet hook: Size G (4.50 mm) or size that gives you correct gauge.

GAUGE

Each large granny square measures 3¼".

STITCHES

Ch, sl st, sc, dc

Degree of difficulty: ****

DIRECTIONS

Note: Work all rnds from right side unless otherwise indicated.

Multicolored Granny Squares

Make 63. Starting at center with color C, ch 4.

Rnd 1: In 4th ch from hook, work 2 dc, ch 1, (3 dc, ch 1) 3 times; join with sl st in top of ch 3. Fasten off.

Rnd 2: Join B to any ch-1 sp, ch 3, (2 dc, ch 1, 3 dc) in same sp (first corner made), * ch 1, (3 dc, ch 1, 3 dc) in next ch-1 sp (another corner made); repeat from * twice more, ch 1; join. Fasten off.

Rnd 3: Join any bright color to any corner, work first corner as before, * ch 1, 3 dc in next ch-1 sp, ch 1, work corner in corner ch-1 sp; repeat from * around, ending last repeat with ch 1; join. Fasten off.

Black-and-White Granny Squares

Make 36. Work same as for multicolored squares, working Rnd 1 with A, Rnd 2 with B, and Rnd 3 with A.

Center Panel

Assembly: Arrange multicolored squares to form panel of 9 rows of 7 squares each, scattering colors throughout. Working from wrong side, join squares, crocheting sl st through back lps of corresponding edge sts.

Panel inner edging: *Rnd 1 (designer's method):* Join A to sp at any panel corner, ch 3 (counts as first dc), * sk 1 dc, dc in next 2 dc, dc in next ch-1 sp, (dc in next 3 dc, dc in next ch-1 sp) twice; dc in corner sp of next square; repeat from * around panel, working 3 dc at panel corners and adding dc on sides if needed to keep edge flat; end with 2 dc in first sp; join to top of ch 3, turn. *Alternate method for Rnd 1:* Join A to sp at any panel corner, ch 3 (counts as first dc), * working in back lp only, (dc in next 3 dc, dc in next ch) 3 times, dc in corner sp of next square; repeat from * around panel, working 3 dc at panel corners and ending with 2 dc in first sp; join to top of ch 3, turn. *Rnd 2 (wrong side):* Dc in each dc around, working 3 dc in center dc at corners. Fasten off.

Panel border: With A, join black-and-white squares with sl st to form 2 strips of 7 squares each and 2 strips of 9 squares each. With A, work a row of dc across each end of each strip. With sl st join strips to corresponding sides of center panel, leaving corners open. Sl st a square to each corner to complete border.

Second edging: *Rnd 1:* With A, working in back lp only throughout edging, dc in each st around panel, working 3 dc at corners. Fasten off. *Rnd 2:* With B, repeat last rnd. *Rnd 3:* Join A to first corner on a short

end of panel, ch 3, * (dc, ch 1, sk 1 st) along short edge, 3 dc in corner, dc in each dc on long edge, 3 dc in corner; repeat from * once more, ending with 2 dc in first corner; join. *Rnd 4:* Ch 3, dc in each st on short edge, 3 dc in corner, work (dc in 2 dc, ch 1, sk 1 dc) on long edge, 3 dc in corner; repeat from * once more, ending with 2 dc in first corner; join. Fasten off.

Small Squares (for panel ends)

Make 26. Work Rnds 1 and 2 same as for black-and-white squares, omitting Rnd 3. With A, sc in back lp only of each ch and dc on one edge of square (9 sc). Fasten off. Repeat on opposite side of square. Joining along A edges, with A, sew pieces together through back lps of sc to form 2 strips of 13 squares each. Center and sew a strip across each short end of afghan. Add to length if necessary by crocheting rows of sc with A on each strip end until it is same length as short edge of afghan.

Afghan Border

Rnd 1: With A, dc in back lp of each st around afghan, working 3 dc at corners; join. Fasten off. With B, working along one long edge, crochet (dc in back lps of 3 dc, ch 1, sk 1 st) along edge. Fasten off. Repeat on opposite long edge.

Rnd 2: With B, dc in each st, working 3 dc at corners; join. Fasten off.

Rnd 3: With C, * work 3 dc at corner, dc in next 2 dc, (sk 2 dc, 3 dc in next dc) across; repeat from * around, working 2 dc before corner (or adjusting number of dc before and after corner as necessary to accommodate pattern); join. Fasten off.

Rnd 4: Repeat Rnd 2.

Rnd 5: With A, repeat Rnd 2.

Rnd 6: With D, repeat Rnd 3.

Rnds 7 and 8: With A, repeat Rnd 2.

Rnd 9: Join B 2 sts before a corner, sc in same st, sk 1 st, work 5 dc in corner st, * sk 1 st, sc in next st, sk 1 st, work 3 dc in next st; repeat from * around, working corners as before. Fasten off.

Delicate Diskettes

Different-sized "granny rounds,"
beautifully laced together, make
this design an eye-catching delight
and a third-prize winner.

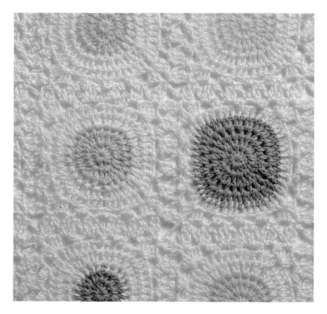

Marietta Jensen
Grand Junction, Colorado

Marietta Jensen is a busy grandmother of eight who works full time as a bookkeeper for Woolworth's. An active bowler and golfer, she's not the sort who sits around with empty hands. Much of her spare time is spent crocheting gifts for members of her family.

This dainty baby quilt was made for her granddaughter. Marietta wanted to use colorful rounds rather than squares, but couldn't find such a pattern anywhere. So she made up a "granny round"—a square with a disk at the center. The units are held together by a white chain stitch, worked around the lacy edges of the squares.

SIZE
About 38″ × 46″

MATERIALS
Yarn: Knitting worsted, 24 oz. white (MC); 3½ oz. each pink (P) and blue (B); 2½ oz. each yellow (Y) and mint green (G).

Crochet hook: Size I (5.50 mm) or size that gives you correct gauge.

GAUGE
Each square measures 6¼″ across.

STITCHES
Ch, sl st, sc, dc

Degree of difficulty: ****

Note: Work all rnds from right side.

DIRECTIONS
Basic Square
Make 42 in all.

Note: Squares are made with color on first 2, 3, or 4 rnds, then completed in MC. See Assembly Diagram, Figure 1, to determine how many rnds of which color to use for each square.

Starting at center with desired color, ch 4. Join with sl st to form ring.

Rnd 1: Ch 3 (counts as first dc), work 11 dc in ring; join to top of ch 3.

Rnd 2: Ch 3, dc in sp between ch 3 and next dc, work 2 dc in each sp between 2 dc around (24 dc counting ch 3); join. (For squares with 2-rnd colored center, fasten off color and join MC.)

Rnd 3: Ch 3 (counts as first dc), sk sp between ch 3 and first dc, work (dc in next sp between 2 dc) around (24 dc); join. (For squares with 3-rnd color center, fasten off color and join MC.)

Rnd 4: Ch 3, dc in first sp between ch 3 and dc, work (2 dc in next sp between 2 dc) around (48 dc); join. (For squares with 4-rnd colored center, fasten off color and join MC.)

Rnd 5: Ch 4, sk sp between ch 3 and dc, (dc in next 12 sp, ch 1) 3 times, dc in last 11 sp; join to 3rd ch of ch 4.

Rnd 6: Ch 3, work (2 dc, ch 2, 3 dc) in ch-1 sp (first corner made), * ch 2, sk 2 sp between dc, work (sc, ch 5, sc) in next sp (picot made); repeat from * twice more, ch 2, sk 2 sp, work (3 dc, ch 2, 3 dc) in ch-1 sp (another corner made) **; repeat from * to ** around, ending last repeat with ch 2; join to top of ch 3. Fasten off.

Assembly
Lay out squares, following Assembly Diagram.

Zigzag joining: Holding 2 squares with wrong sides together, attach MC to corner ch-2 sp of one square, ch 3, sc in corresponding corner sp of 2nd square, ch 3, sc in same corner sp of first square, ch 3, sc in same corner sp of 2nd square, * ch 3, sc in next ch-2 sp of first square, ch 3, sc in corresponding ch-2 sp of 2nd square, ch 3, sc in same sp on first square, ch 3, sc in same ch-2 sp of 2nd square; continue in this manner back and forth between squares, always working ch 3 between sc and working 2 sc in each ch-2 sp along edges to next corner, working (ch 3, sc) twice in corners. Fasten off. Join squares in strips, then join strips in same manner.

Border
With right side of work facing you, attach MC to ch-2 sp at any corner of afghan.

Rnd 1: Work sc in same sp, * ch 3, work (sc, ch 5, sc) in next ch-2 sp (picot made); repeat from * around, ending with sc in first sp, ch 5; join to first sc to complete corner picot.

Rnd 2: Sl st in first ch of next ch 3, picot in same sp, work (ch 3, picot in next sp) around, ending ch 3; join to first sc of first picot. Fasten off.

3G	3P	4B	4Y	3B	4P
4B	2G	3Y	3G	2P	3Y
3Y	4P	2B	3P	4G	3B
2P	3Y	3G	4B	2Y	3P
4G	3B	2P	3Y	4P	2G
3P	3G	4Y	2G	3B	3Y
4B	2Y	3B	4P	3G	3P

Figure 1. Assembly Diagram

Milles Fleurs

This very traditional granny afghan, distinguished by
the use of explosive colors and superb execution,
is perfect for an adventurous beginner.

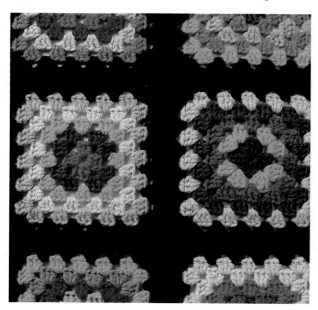

Kathleen Delaney Kenyon
Priest River, Idaho

Kathleen not only crochets (this is her tenth afghan), she also creates
twig-and-straw wreaths, baskets, ceramic Christmas ornaments, cornhusk
and fabric dolls, hand-dipped candles, and "who knows what's next!"

Besides crafts, Kathleen's indoor passion is cooking on her wood-
burning stove, filling cold wintry days with the "cheery crackle of a fire
and the aroma of hot coffee or baking bread."

But these pleasures "take a back seat to my outdoor chores. We live
in northern Idaho, surrounded by mountains and U.S. National Forest,
with the luxury of a telephone, but no electricity." In addition to growing
flowers and vegetables, the Kenyons raise their own beef, keep chickens
and a registered Alpine dairy goat, "which produces the cream for my
husband's favorite butterscotch cream pie."

Kathleen learned to crochet from a friend in Alaska, where she lived
ten years ago. She thereupon taught her mother. "My most treasured
afghan," she says, "is the one she made for me."

SIZE
About 60" × 78"

MATERIALS
Yarn: Knitting worsted, 26 oz. black, 70 oz. assorted colors (see Note below).

Crochet hook: Size I (5.50 mm) or size that gives you correct gauge.

GAUGE
Each square measures 6" across.

STITCHES
Ch, sl st, sc, dc

Degree of difficulty: *

DIRECTIONS
Note: Designer used 4 to 5 oz. each of 15 different colors in shades of blue, purple, and red. She changed color for each rnd and made each square different by varying order of colors used. Save scrap ends of colored yarn (1 yd. or more) to use in border.

Work all rnds from right side.

Squares
Make 108. Starting at center with first color, ch 4. Join with sl st to form ring.

Rnd 1: Ch 3 (counts as first dc), work 2 dc in ring, ch 3, (3 dc in ring, ch 3) 3 times; join with sl st to top of starting ch 3. Fasten off. Attach next color to any corner ch-3 lp.

Rnd 2: Ch 3, (2 dc, ch 3, 3 dc) over same lp (first corner made), ch 1, * (3 dc, ch 3, 3 dc) over next corner lp (another corner made), ch 1; repeat from * around; join. Fasten off. Attach next color to any corner lp.

Rnd 3: Work first corner as before, * ch 1, work 3 dc in next ch-1 sp, ch 1, work another corner; repeat from * around, ending with 3 dc in last sp, ch 1; join. Fasten off. Attach next color to any corner lp.

Rnd 4: *Work corner, ch 1, (3 dc, ch 1) in each ch-1 sp to next corner; repeat from * around; join. Fasten off. Attach next color to any corner lp.

Rnd 5: Repeat Rnd 4.

Rnd 6: With black, repeat Rnd 4, but do not fasten off.

Rnd 7: Ch 1, sc in back lp only of each dc and ch around; join to first sc. Fasten off.

Assembly
Arrange squares as desired to form rectangle 9 squares by 12 squares. Join squares, sewing through back lps of corresponding sts along adjoining edges.

Border
Attach black yarn to back loop of sc at any afghan corner.

Rnd 1: Ch 3, working in back lp only throughout, dc in same st, * dc in each st to next corner, 4 dc in corner st; repeat from * around to first corner, work 2 more dc in first corner; join to top of ch 3.

Rnd 2: Repeat Rnd 1. Fasten off.

Rnd 3: (**Note:** Use scrap yarns in 1- to 5-yd. lengths, changing colors at end of each strand by working last st of old color until last 2 lps remain on hook, then with new yarn, yo and draw through lps to complete st.) Attach first color strand and sc in back lp of each st around, changing colors and working 3 sc at each corner; join.

Rnds 4 and 5: Work same as Rnd 3, varying colors. See that color changes do not lie directly above previous changes.

Rnd 6: Attach black yarn to any corner, then repeat Rnd 1.

Rnd 7: Ch 1, sc in back lp of each dc around, working 3 sc at corners. Fasten off.

Baby Pie

Dainty pie-shaped units are
pieced together to make
a delightful baby quilt.

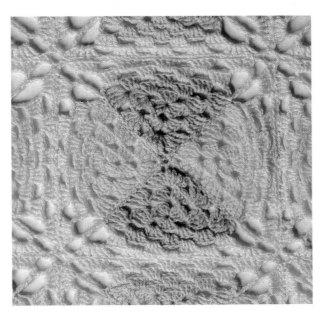

Ruth M. Nelson
Dugway, Utah

This busy mother of three young boys recently gave up teaching full
time to spend more time with her family. Ruth loves all kinds of needlework and is proficient in sewing, knitting, needlepoint, and embroidery
as well as crocheting. Her mother was always engaged in some kind of
craft work so, she feels, "it rubbed off on me."

But the particular source of inspiration for the pie-shaped pastel units
that make up this soft, lacy baby quilt was her grandmother. "I used to
watch her make star design quilts out of different colors of material—
they were so beautiful. When I learned to crochet, I would think about
the quilts she made, and I wanted to crochet a blanket that looked like
her quilts."

Ruth does some volunteer teaching as an exercise instructor four days
a week, and is a director for the Salt Lake Women's Bowling Associa-
tion. So she managed to complete her afghan by crocheting on her trips
to town—forty-five miles away.

SIZE
About 40″ square

MATERIALS
Yarn: Sport yarn, 7 oz. white (color A), 2½ oz. peach (B), 2 oz. lavender (C); 3 oz. each yellow (D) and mint green (E); 2 oz. each blue (F) and pink (G).

Crochet hook: Size G (4.50 mm) or size that gives you correct gauge.

GAUGE
Each square measures 7½″ across.

STITCHES
Ch, sl st, sc, hdc, dc, tr

Degree of difficulty: ****

DIRECTIONS
Note: Each square unit is made of 4 colored triangles sewn together to form a center circle with white border crocheted around.

Work all rnds from right side.

Triangles
Make 10 each with B and C, 16 each with F and G, 24 each with D and E. Starting at center with desired color, ch 4. Join with sl st to form ring.

Rnd 1: Ch 3, 3 dc in ring, (ch 4, 4 dc) twice, ch 4; join with sl st to top of ch 3.

Rnd 2: Sl st to first ch-4 lp, ch 3, work (3 dc, ch 4, 4 dc) over first ch-4 lp (first point made), ch 1, work (4 tr, ch 4, 4 dc) over next lp (2nd point made), ch 1, (4 dc, ch 4, 4 tr) over next lp (3rd point made), ch 1; join to top of ch 3.

Rnd 3: Sl st to next lp, ch 4, (3 tr, ch 3, 4 tr) over same lp (mark for first point), ch 1, 4 tr over next lp, ch 1, (4 tr, ch 4, 4 dc) over next lp, ch 1, 4 dc over next lp, ch 1, (4 dc, ch 4, 4 tr) over next lp, ch 1, 4 tr over next lp, ch 1; join to top of ch 4. Fasten off.

Squares
Make 5 squares with B and C triangles (square 1 on Assembly Diagram, Figure 2), 8 squares with F and G (square 2), 12 squares with D and E (square 3). Alternating colors and sewing through back lps only of corresponding sts, sew together 4 triangles (2 of each color) with marked first points meeting at center and dc edge at outer edge (edge cups slightly.)

Border: *Rnd 1:* Attach A to first lp after any joining, ch 3, 3 dc over same lp, * (ch 2, 4 hdc over next lp) twice, ch 2, 4 dc over next lp, ch 5, tr in joining, ch 5 (corner made), 4 dc over next lp; repeat from * around, ending with ch 5; join to top of ch 3. *Rnd 2:* Sl st to next lp, ch 3, 3 dc over same lp, (ch 2, 4 dc over next lp) twice, * ch 2, 5 dc over next lp, ch 3, 5 dc over next lp, (ch 2, 4 dc over next lp) 3 times; repeat from * around, ending with 5 dc over last lp, ch 2; join. Fasten off.

Assembly
Following Assembly Diagram, sew squares together, sewing through back lps only of corresponding sts.

Border
Rnd 1: Attach A to lp at any corner of afghan, ch 3, work 3 dc over same lp, * work (ch 2, 4 dc over next lp) to next corner, ch 2, (4 dc, ch 3, 4 dc) over corner lp; repeat from * around, ending with (4 dc, ch 3) in first corner lp; join to top of ch 3.

Rnd 2: Ch 5, * work (4 dc over next lp, ch 2) to next corner, (4 dc, ch 3, 4 dc) over corner lp, ch 2; repeat from * around, ending (4 dc, ch 3, 3 dc) in first corner lp; join to 3rd ch of ch 5. Fasten off.

Rnd 3: Attach B to any st, sc in each dc and ch around, working (3 sc, ch 1, 3 sc) over each corner lp; join to first sc.

Rnd 4: Sc in each sc, working 3 sc in each corner ch-1 sp; join. Fasten off.

Rnd 5: Attach C to any sc and sc in each sc around; join. Fasten off.

1	3	2	3	1
3	2	3	2	3
2	3	1	3	2
3	2	3	2	3
1	3	2	3	1

Figure 2. Assembly Diagram

Shadows Over the Rainbow

Inspired by the great outdoors,
this magnificent bedspread will bring
the colors of nature into your home.

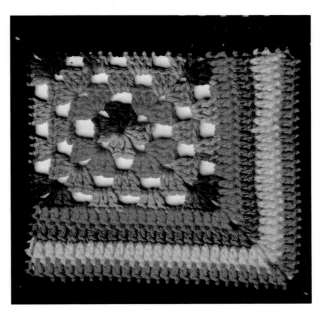

Janice Koci
Diamondville, Wyoming

Janice and her husband live on a fourteen-acre mini-ranch where they keep horses, dogs, cats, and goats. A knitter and crocheter for the past fifty years, she completed this bedspread during the winter months, between ranch chores.

Her inspiration for the colors and the diamond design, whose carefully detailed arrangement forms triangular edges, comes from a love of the great outdoors. She envisioned a chevron rainbow over the traditional granny square, "casting a shadow of black to surround all the colors." Using a traditional background of black, Janice worked out her unique motif with a group of romantic colors she saw in the evening sky and the fields around her: rose, blue, grenadine, turquoise, lavender, sugar and spice. Then she added dashes of leftover yarn, providing the random colors of a meadow filled with wildflowers.

SIZE

About 60″ × 86″

MATERIALS

Yarn: Knitting worsted, 35 oz. black (MC), 50 oz. assorted colors (designer used mostly pinks, blues, and lavender, with some variegated shades).

Crochet hook: Size G (4.50 mm) or size that gives you correct gauge.

GAUGE

Each large square measures 9½″ across.

STITCHES

Ch, sl st, sc, dc

Degree of difficulty: ***

DIRECTIONS

Note: Work all rnds from right side. For best results, use knitting worsted yarn of uniform thickness throughout. If work ripples slightly when you add rainbow rows, use smaller hook to keep work flat.

Large Squares

Make 38. **Note:** Work different color as desired for each of first 4 rnds; repeat at least 1 or 2 of these colors as you work rainbow rows.

Granny square: Starting at center with first color, ch 5. Join with sl st to form ring. **Rnd 1:** Ch 3 (counts as first dc), work 2 dc in ring, ch 2, (3 dc in ring, ch 2) 3 times; join with sl st in top of ch 3. Fasten off. **Rnd 2:** Join new color in any ch-2 sp, ch 3, (2 dc, ch 2, 3 dc) in same sp (first corner made), ch 2, * work (3 dc, ch 2, 3 dc) in next corner sp, ch 2; repeat from * around; join to top of ch 3. Fasten off. **Rnd 3:** Join new color in any corner sp and work first corner as before, ch 2, * 3 dc in next ch-2 sp, ch 2, work corner in next corner sp, ch 2; repeat from * around; join. Fasten off. **Rnd 4:** Attach new color to any corner sp and work first corner, ch 2, * (3 dc in next ch-2 sp, ch 2) twice, work corner, ch 2; repeat from * around; join. Fasten off.

Rainbow: Row 1: Attach next color in any corner sp, ch 3, * work dc in each dc and 2 dc in each ch-2 sp to next corner sp **, work (2 dc, ch 2, 2 dc) in corner sp; repeat from * to **, work 1 dc in corner sp (2 sides of square worked). Fasten off. **Rows 2 through 4:** Attach next color to top of starting ch 3 of last row, work dc in each dc to next corner sp, work (2 dc, ch 2, 2 dc) in corner sp, dc in each dc to end of last row. Fasten off.

Shadow: Next rnd: Attach MC to unworked corner sp of granny-square section, ch 3, work (dc, ch 2, 2 dc) in same sp, work dc in each dc and 2 dc in each ch-2 sp to start of rainbow stripes, ending with 1 dc in corner sp of granny square, then work 2 dc into side edge of each of first 3 stripes, work 1 dc into next stripe row, work (2 dc, ch 2, 2 dc) in top of ch-3, * dc in each dc to next corner, work (2 dc, ch 2, 2 dc) in corner; repeat from * once more; work 1 dc into side edge of first stripe row, work 2 dc in each remaining stripe, dc in corner sp of granny square, work dc in each dc and 2 dc in each ch-2 sp to end; join to top of ch 3. Do not fasten off. **Next rnd:** Ch 3, dc in each dc around, working (2 dc, ch 2, 2 dc) in each corner sp; join. Fasten off.

Half-Squares (triangles for side edges of afghan)

Make 12.

Half-granny square: With first color, ch 4. *Row 1:* In 4th ch from hook, work (2 dc, ch 2, 3 dc) for corner. Fasten off. *Row 2:* Join new color to top of starting ch 3, ch 3, work 2 dc in same place, ch 2, work (3 dc, ch 2, 3 dc) in corner sp, ch 2, 3 dc in last dc. Fasten off. *Row 3:* Attach next color to top of ch 3, ch 3, work 2 dc in same place, ch 2, 3 dc in next sp, ch 2, work corner in corner sp, ch 2, 3 dc in next sp, ch 2, 3 dc in last dc. Fasten off. *Row 4:* Attach next color to top of ch 3, ch 3, work 2 dc in same place, ch 2, (3 dc in next sp, ch 2) twice, work corner, ch 2, (3 dc in next sp, ch 2) twice, 3 dc in last dc. Fasten off.

Rainbow for 6 A half-squares: Work the 6 half-squares shown as A on Assembly Diagram, Figure 3, as follows: *Row 1:* Attach next color to top of ch 3, work dc in each dc and 2 dc in each sp across one side to next corner sp, work 2 dc in corner sp. Fasten off. *Rows 2 through 4:* Attach next color to top of ch 3, dc in each dc across. Fasten off.

Rainbow for 6 B half-squares: Work the 6 half-squares shown as B on Assembly Diagram as follows: *Row 1:* Attach next color to corner lp, dc in same lp, work dc in each dc and 2 dc in each sp across one side to end. Fasten off. Complete to correspond to A half-squares.

Shadow (for all half-squares): *Next rnd:* Attach MC to top of starting ch 3, work dc in each dc, 2 dc in each sp and side edge of each stripe row all around half-square, working (2 dc, ch 2, 2 dc) at each point; join. *Next rnd:* Ch 3, dc in each dc around, working (2 dc, ch 2, 2 dc) in sp at each point; join. Fasten off.

Small Granny Squares (C on Assembly Diagram)

Make 8.

Rnds 1 and 2: Work same as Rnds 1 and 2 of large squares.

Rnd 3: Attach MC to any corner sp, work 2 sc in each sp (including corners), and sc in each dc around; join to first sc. Fasten off.

Assembly

Following Assembly Diagram, lay out pieces with rainbow stripes on each square and half-square toward bottom edge of afghan.

Joining: Starting with A half-square at upper left corner, attach MC to point (marked 1 on diagram), ch 3, sc in same place, * ch 3, sk 1 st, sc in next st; repeat from * around, working (sc, ch 3, sc) in sp at each point (looped border worked around piece). Fasten off. Join each new unit, working (ch 3, sk 1 st, sc in next st) around free edges and joining edges that touch previously worked units as follows: Work sc in corner sp of previous unit, * work (ch 3, sk 1 st, sc in next st) on new unit, ch 3, sc in next ch-3 lp on previous unit; repeat from * across, ending with sc in corner sp of previous unit. Continue in this manner until all units, including small squares (C) at ends, are joined.

Afghan Border

Join MC to sp at any corner of afghan, work (ch 3, sc over next lp) all around afghan, working (sc, ch 3, sc) in each corner and outer point. Fasten off. With MC, work 2 more rows of (ch 3, sc over next lp) along each side edge of afghan.

Fringe: For each fringe, cut ten 10″ strands of assorted colors (omitting MC) and make fringe (see page 165) where indicated on diagram at each indentation along top and bottom edges.

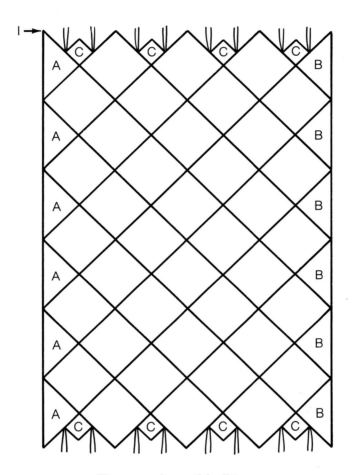

Figure 3. Assembly Diagram

Unmarked units = Whole squares

A and B units = Half-squares

C units = Small granny squares

Baby Broomstick Lace

Tiny granny squares bordered with
broomstick lace make this the
sweetest carriage cover in town.

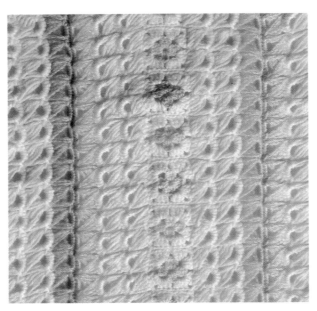

Georgia A. Shaulis
Somerset, Pennsylvania

This light and airy carriage cover made of tiny granny squares is sure
to stir envy in the heart of every new mother in the neighborhood.
Georgia began it as soon as she found out she was expecting her second
child and finished it the night before he was born. She "wanted to make
something very special to welcome this new little life into mine."

Having been taught to crochet by her mother when she was fourteen,
she knew all the basic stitches and could experiment with her own designs and placement of stitches. The delicate look of broomstick lace
with granny motifs seemed perfect for the expected arrival.

Crocheting has grown from a hobby into a way of life for Georgia. In
addition to her work as a computer operator, she teaches crocheting at
the local arts center and has begun a Crochet Arts Guild, which is about
to expand to the national level.

SIZE

About 27″ × 35″

MATERIALS

Yarn: Baby yarn, 10 oz. white (MC); baby yarn with glitter thread (such as Coats and Clark Red Heart Pompadour), 1 oz. each light green (color A), peach (B), baby blue (C), baby pink (D), yellow (E).

Crochet hook: Size E (3.50 mm) or size that gives you correct gauge; broomstick lace pin (also called Jiffy Lace needle), size 35 (¾″ diameter), or see Note below.

GAUGE

Each square measures 1½″ across.

STITCHES

Ch, sl st, sc, dc, broomstick lace (directions given below)

Degree of difficulty: ****

DIRECTIONS

Note: Afghan is made of strips of granny squares, bordered with broomstick lace, then joined, with afghan border added. If you have difficulty finding a lace pin, you can make your own: Sand one end of an 18″-long, ¾″-diameter dowel into a smooth tapered point and wrap a rubber band several times around other end to keep sts from slipping off.

Granny Squares

Make 20 with A center, 15 each with B, C, D, and E center. Starting at center with desired color, ch 4. Join with sl st to form ring.

Rnd 1 (right side): Ch 5 (counts as first dc and ch-2 lp), work (3 dc in ring, ch 2) 3 times, 2 dc in ring; join with sl st to 3rd

ch of ch 5. Fasten off color; attach MC to center of any ch-2 lp.

Rnd 2: On right side of work, ch 5, 3 dc over same lp, * ch 1, work (3 dc, ch 2, 3 dc) over next lp; repeat from * twice more, ch 1, 2 dc over first lp; join with sl st to 3rd ch of ch 5. Fasten off MC.

Granny Square Strips

Join 16 squares each in 5 strips, sewing squares together through back lps and arranging colors on each strip as follows: A, then (B, C, D, E, A) 3 times.

Broomstick Lace Borders

Work 1 strip each with A, B, C, D, or E on last row. (**Note:** If you have never worked broomstick lace before, practice first until you feel comfortable working it.) With right side of work facing you, attach MC to beg of one long edge of strip. Hold broomstick lace pin in left hand just behind top of work.

Row 1: *First half:* With crochet hook, draw up long lp in ch of corner lp and place on lace pin, continue to draw up lp in each dc, ch, and joining across, draw up extra lp in last square (10 lps each square—160 lps in all), placing each lp on lace pin as it is made. Note that work hanging from pin is turned with wrong side facing you. *Second half:* With wrong side of squares facing you, insert crochet hook right to left through first 5 lps on lace pin (at center top of lps), yo and draw through 5 lps and lp on hook, ch 1 to hold lps tog, sl these 5 lps off pin and work 5 sc over center of lps, * insert hook through next 5 lps on pin, ch 1 to hold lps tog, sl lps off pin and work 5 sc over center of lps; repeat from * across (160 sc). Turn work.

Row 2: In each sc across, draw up lp and place on lace pin as for Row 1, always skipping ch 1 between 5-sc groups; work off as for 2nd half of Row 1. Fasten off MC and attach desired color.

Row 3: Repeat Row 2. Fasten off. Work 3 broomstick lace rows on opposite side of strip to correspond. Work each strip in same manner, changing color for last row.

Assembly

Holding right sides together, sl st edges of strips together.

Afghan Border

With MC, work 1 row of broomstick lace along each long edge, picking up 200 lps evenly spaced along each edge; work 1 row of broomstick lace across each short edge, picking up 170 lps. Work 1 sc row each of D, C, B, A, and E all around afghan, working 3 sc at each corner on each row.

Baby Valentines

**Eight little hearts surround the
center of this square, creating an ideal
pattern for a baby blanket.**

Talla Sjaaheim
Valparaiso, Indiana

Talla began her afghan around Valentine's Day, so she knew she
"wanted something with a heart shape in it." The centers of these
charming squares are tilted on the bias with the hearts formed by crocheted chains. The crisp white background provides a gentle contrast to
the soft pastel shades.

Talla's mother taught her how to crochet when she was twelve and
she has been doing it ever since. She also enjoys knitting and macramé.

Talla, who works part time filling orders at a warehouse, didn't have
any particular baby in mind when she began her afghan. But she does
now. She became pregnant with her first child soon after she entered
the contest.

SIZE

Each square measures 5½″ across. To make an afghan of the size you desire, see page 165, Designing on Your Own.

MATERIALS

Yarn: Knitting worsted; *for each square:* 11 yd. white (color A); 2 yd. each light blue (B), light yellow (C), light green (D), light pink (E), plus additional 5 yd. desired border color (B, C, D, or E). See page 166 for how to estimate amount of yarn needed for an afghan.

Crochet hook: Size H (5.00 mm) or size that gives you correct gauge.

STITCHES

Ch, sl st, sc, dc, tr

Degree of difficulty: ****

DIRECTIONS

Note: Work in back lp only of sts throughout. Work all rnds from right side.

Squares

Starting at center with color A, ch 6. Join with sl st to form ring.

Rnd 1: Ch 3 (counts as first dc), 2 dc in ring, (ch 3, 3 dc in ring) 3 times, ch 3; join with sl st to top of ch 3. Fasten off.

Rnd 2 (heart rnd): * Attach B to center dc of one 3-dc group, ch 10, sl st in 2nd ch from hook (picot made), ch 8, sl st in same place where color was joined (loop for heart

made); fasten off B; in same manner, make C heart loop in center of next ch-3 corner lp, make D heart loop in center dc of next 3-dc group, make E heart loop in center of next ch-3 corner lp; repeat from * once more (8 heart loops).

Rnd 3: Attach A to 7th ch of first B heart loop, ch 3, 2 dc in same ch, * sk (ch, picot, and ch), work 3 dc in next ch, sk 1 ch, work tr to join hearts by yo twice, then insert hook in next ch, then through 5th ch of next adjoining heart lp, complete tr, sk 1 ch on new heart, work 3 dc in next ch, sk (ch, picot, and ch), work 3 dc in next ch, ch 3, sk 1 ch, work tr to join hearts as above, inserting hook through next ch, then 5th ch of next heart, ch 3 (corner made), sk 1 ch on new heart, 3 dc in next ch; repeat from * around, ending with tr through last and first hearts, ch 3; join to top of starting ch 3. Fasten off A; attach desired border color (B, C, D, or E).

Rnd 4: Working in back lp, sc in each st around, working 3 sc in each corner tr; join to first sc. Fasten off.

Joining

To join squares for this afghan, the designer worked from the right side with color A to sc through back lps only of corresponding sts along edges. This joining forms a ridge on the right side of the afghan.

Heart to Heart

In this ingenious design,
the dazzling white connecting stitches
link dancing hearts to form
a larger heart in the center.

Darcee R. Yates
Orem, Utah

This mother of four had the best motivation possible for her prizewinning heart afghan in pinks and burgundies: two little girls, ages 4½ and 8.

Darcee wanted to make an afghan to complement the comforters they already had on their beds, so she chose lavender, pink, and burgundy. The heart design "just seemed the most appropriate for the little girls." While glancing through magazines in search of a pattern for the heart, Darcee came across the contest announcement and decided to enter. She tried a dozen or more designs, experimented with different yarns, colors, and hook sizes, and eventually "came up with the plump heart shape I felt was right."

Darcee never entered a contest before and declares she is absolutely "thrilled at the recognition."

SIZE

About 54″ × 60″

MATERIALS

Yarn: Bulky weight (such as Phentex Chunky), 30 oz. burgundy (color A); 6 oz. each rose (B) and lavender (C); 9 oz. purple (D), 18 oz. white (E).

Crochet hook: Size I (5.50 mm) or size that gives you correct gauge.

GAUGE

Heart, with border, measures 4¾″ across and 4″ from top to bottom.

STITCHES

Ch, sl st, sc, hdc, dc, tr

Degree of difficulty: ***

DIRECTIONS

Note: Work all rnds from right side.

Hearts

Make 124 with color A, 18 each with B and C, 24 with D. Starting at center with desired color (A, B, C, or D), ch 6. Join with sl st to form ring.

Rnd 1: Ch 3 (counts as first dc), dc in ring, ch 2, (2 dc in ring, ch 2) 5 times; join with sl st to top of ch 3.

Rnd 2: Work (ch 2, dc, tr) in same place as joining, tr in next dc, 7 tr in next ch-2 sp, sk 1 dc, work (dc, hdc) in next dc, 2 sc in next sp, sk 1 dc, sc in next dc, work (sc, ch 1, dc, ch 1, sc) in next sp (bottom point made), sc in next dc, sk 1 dc, 2 sc in next sp, (hdc, dc) in next dc, sk 1 dc, 7 tr in next sp, tr in next dc, (tr, dc, ch 2) in last dc; sl st in next sp. Fasten off.

Rnd 3 (border): Attach E to starting ch 2, sc over same lp, sc in dc, sc in tr, 2 hdc in each of next 2 sts, (hdc in next st, 2 hdc in next st) twice, sc in next 8 sts, sk 1 sc, sc in next dc (at point), sk 1 ch, sc in next 8 sts, (2 hdc in next st, hdc in next st) twice, 2 hdc in each of next 2 sts, sc in tr, sc in dc, sc over ch 2; join to first sc. Fasten off.

Assembly

Following Assembly Diagram, Figure 4, for placement, sew adjoining edges of hearts, working sl st through back lps only of corresponding sts and leaving small open areas along line where tops of hearts meet as shown.

Border

Attach A to any st along afghan edge.

Rnd 1: Work hdc around, working 2 hdc in sts around outwardly curved edges to make slightly ruffled edge.

Rnds 2 and 3: Work 2 more rnds of hdc in each hdc around. Fasten off.

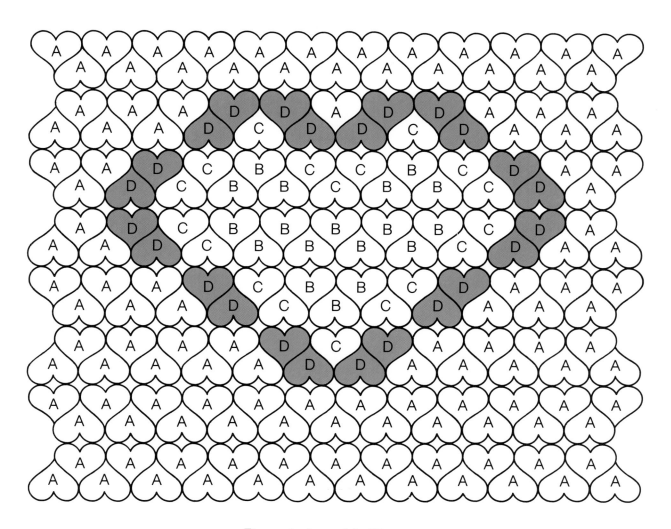

Figure 4. Assembly Diagram

Lacy Lattice

These exquisite little granny squares
are connected as they are worked,
a great timesaver.

Mary Swartz
Indianola, Nebraska

This mother of three girls has been crocheting for over twenty years. Taught by her mother when she was nine or ten, she in turn has taught all her daughters, even the six-year-old, to crochet. Her ten-year-old has great fun creating afghans for her dolls.

Mary works full time as cook and housekeeper for her parish priest but still finds spare hours to crochet potholders, toys, dolls, doll clothes, sweaters, dresses, vests, Christmas ornaments, purses, pillows, and afghans for friends and family.

When Mary found out her sister was expecting her first baby, she wanted to make a baby quilt. But "not being a quilter, I decided to see how one would look in crochet." The quiltlike lattice pattern is created by deft changes in her yarn colors.

SIZE

About 35" × 44"

MATERIALS

Yarn: Sturdy-quality baby yarn (such as Lion Brand Jamie, with glitter thread, if desired), 5 oz. each white (W), pink (P), yellow (Y), blue (B), and green (G).

Crochet hook: Size F (4.00 mm) or size that gives you correct gauge.

GAUGE

Each square measures about 1⅛" across.

STITCHES

Ch, sl st, dc

Degree of difficulty: **

DIRECTIONS

Note: Afghan is worked in small squares joined together as you go.

Afghan

Start at one corner of afghan.

Row 1 of afghan: *First square:* Starting at center with Y, ch 4. Join with sl st to form ring. Right side: Ch 3 (counts as first dc), work 2 dc in ring, (ch 3, 3 dc in ring) 3 times, ch 3; join with sl st to top of ch 3. Fasten off. *Second square:* With P, work as for first square until three 3-dc sides are completed; for corner, work ch 1, sl st into a corner of previous square (with right sides facing same way), ch 1 (regular corner joining made), work 3 dc in ring, work corner joining as before in next corner (see Joining Diagrams, Figures 5A and 5B); join to top of starting ch 3. With P, continue to work and join squares until you have strip of 31 squares.

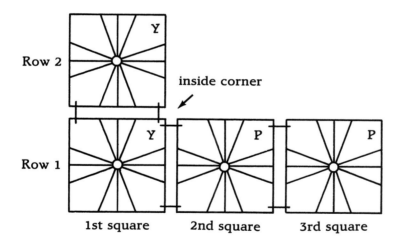

Figure 5A. Joining Diagram

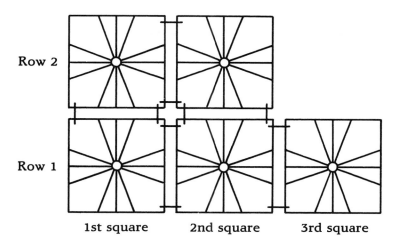

Row 2

Row 1

1st square   2nd square   3rd square

Figure 5B. Joining Diagram

Row 2 of afghan: *First square:* With Y, work and join square to previous Y square (see Joining Diagram). *Second square:* With P, work and join square, joining inside corner formed by 3 previous squares as follows: ch 1, sl st into corner of last square completed, sl st into corner of corresponding square of previous row, ch 1 (this completes inside corner joining).

Continue working squares in rows, joining regular or inside corner joinings as needed and following Color Chart, Figure 6, on page 42, working each row across from *a* to *c* once, repeating from *b* to *c* 6 times, then working *c* to *d* once; work rows from *w* to *y* once; repeat from *x* to *y* 8 times, then work *y* to *z* once. When all rows are completed, fasten off.

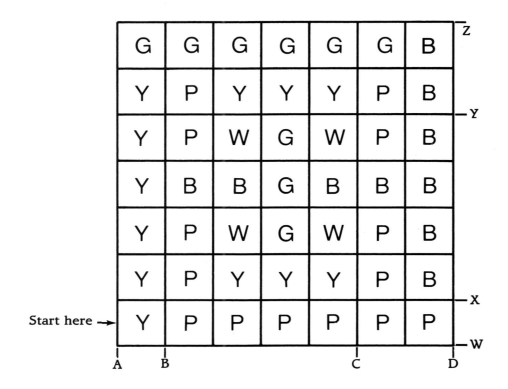

Figure 6. Color Chart

Cathedral Windows

The raised ridges connecting these
gentle, subtle colors evoke
the gridwork of beautiful
stained-glass windows.

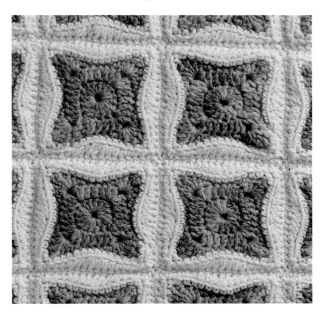

Norma G. Webb
Tallahassee, Florida

Whoever thought the arts and sciences were far apart never met
Norma Webb. A chemist who has been doing fine needlework since she
was twelve years old, Norma gracefully bridges the gap between these
disciplines. In fact, she finds that her interest in one complements and
balances her interest in the other. As assistant chief of the food labora-
tory at the Florida Department of Agriculture and Consumer Services,
her job is technically oriented and mentally demanding. "My crocheting
and other needlework hobbies provide a form of mental diversion and
relaxation that I find necessary to balance my daily activities."

The catalyst for this project was Norma's desire to earn some extra
money for her daughter's upcoming wedding. In fact, this splendid pattern in beige, sand, and blue is her first attempt to create an original design. She based it on her favorite quilt pattern, Cathedral Windows.

SIZE

Each square measures 4½″ across. To make an afghan of the size you desire, see page 165, Designing on Your Own.

MATERIALS

Yarn: Knitting worsted; *for each square:* 10 yd. variegated (color A), 8½ yd. off-white (B). See page 166 for how to estimate amount of yarn needed for an afghan.

Crochet hook: Size H (5.00 mm) or size that gives you correct gauge.

STITCHES

Ch, sl st, sc, hdc, dc, tr

Degree of difficulty: **

DIRECTIONS

Note: Work all rnds from right side.

Square

Starting at center with A, ch 4. Join with sl st to form ring.

Rnd 1: Ch 3 (counts as first dc), 15 dc in ring; join with sl st to top of ch 3.

Rnd 2: Ch 3, * (2 dc, ch 2, 2 dc) in next dc (corner made), dc in next 3 dc; repeat from * around, ending with dc in last 2 dc; join to ch 3.

Rnd 3: Ch 1, sc in top of ch 3, sc in next 2 dc, * (hdc, dc, 2 tr, dc, hdc) over next corner lp, sk first dc, sc in next 6 dc; repeat from * around, ending last repeat with sc in last 3 dc; join to first sc. Fasten off. Fasten B to first dc at any corner.

Rnd 4: Sc in each st around, working 3 sc in 2nd tr at each corner; join to first sc.

Rnd 5: Working in back lp of sts, ch 1, sc in first 3 sc, * (sc, ch 1, sc) in next sc (corner made), sc in next 3 sc, hdc in next 3 sc, dc in next sc, hdc in next 3 sc, sc in next 3 sc; repeat from * around, ending with hdc in last 3 sc; join. Fasten off.

Joining

To join these squares, the designer worked from wrong side to crochet with sl st through *front* lps only of corresponding sts along square edges. This causes square to puff forward slightly, giving squares an interesting 3-D effect.

Desert Landscape

These large, airy squares,
in a palette of southwestern colors,
have a delightful homespun appearance.

Barbara L. Cheyne
Rome, New York

Barbara Cheyne spent only one week of the long, cold winter season in central New York State creating a floral throw in colors that suggest the warmth of a desert landscape. Using her favorite shades of coral, brown, taupe, and steel blue, she fashioned an imaginary springtime. Since she admits to getting bored with small, intricate patterns, she chose bulky yarn that works up fast. This is a project that will appeal to the most impatient crocheter.

Enjoying the flexibility of a housewife's schedule, Barbara is currently researching her Scottish ancestry and attending clan meetings whenever possible, in addition to bicycling, gardening, and painting.

Barbara learned to crochet a few years ago and since then she's been picking up stitches and methods from books and patterns. She confides, "I've always preferred creating my own designs, although I'm sure I've ended up with more ripped-out mistakes than finished products."

SIZE

About 46" × 67"

MATERIALS

Yarn: Bulky weight (such as Phentex Chunky), 6 oz. steel blue (color A), 15 oz. beige (B), 24 oz. taupe (C), and 9 oz. coral (D).

Crochet hooks: Sizes I and J (5.50 and 6.00 mm) or sizes that give you correct gauge.

GAUGE

Each square measures 10½" across.

STITCHES

Ch, sl st, dc, tr, tr tr

Degree of difficulty: **

DIRECTIONS

Note: Work all rnds from right side.

Squares

Make 24. Starting at center with color A and smaller hook, ch 8. Join with sl st to form ring.

Rnd 1: Ch 6, tr tr (see page 163), ch 3, * 2 tr tr, ch 3; repeat from * 6 times more; join to top of ch 6. Fasten off. Change to larger hook.

Rnd 2: Join B to any ch-3 lp, ch 3, work (2 dc, ch 3, 3 dc) over same lp (first corner made), * ch 1, 3 dc over next lp, ch 1, (3 dc, ch 3, 3 dc) over next lp (another corner made); repeat from * around, ending with ch 1; join to top of ch 3. Fasten off.

Rnd 3: Join C to first dc after any corner lp, ch 3 (counts as first dc), sk first dc, * dc in each dc and ch-1 sp to next corner lp, work 5 dc over corner lp; repeat from * around; join. Fasten off.

Rnd 4: Join D to center dc at any corner, ch 5 (counts as first tr and ch 1), work (tr, ch 1) twice more in same dc, * work (sk 1 dc, tr in next dc, ch 1) to center dc of next corner, work (tr, ch 1) 3 times in center dc of corner; repeat from * around, ending with ch 1; join to 4th ch of ch 5. Fasten off.

Rnd 5: Join C to center tr at any corner, ch 3, 4 dc in same tr, * 2 dc in each sp to center tr of next corner, 5 dc in center tr; repeat from * around, ending 2 dc in last sp; join. Fasten off.

Rnd 6: Join B to center dc at any corner, ch 3, 4 dc in same dc, * dc in each dc to center dc at next corner, 5 dc in center dc; repeat from * around, ending dc in last dc; join. Fasten off.

Assembly

Sewing through back lps of corresponding sts along edges, join squares to form panel 4 squares by 6 squares.

Border

Attach B to center dc at any corner.

Rnd 1: Ch 3 (counts as first dc), work 3 more dc in same place (first corner made), then dc in each dc around, working 4 dc at each corner; join to top of ch 3. Fasten off.

Rnd 2: With C repeat Rnd 1. Do not fasten off.

Rnds 3 and 4: Ch 3, working in back lp of sts, dc in each dc around, omitting inc at corners; join.

Rnd 5: Ch 3, working in back lp of sts, dc in each dc around, working corners as follows: Work to last 2 dc before corner dc, (yo and draw up lp in next dc, yo and draw through first 2 lps on hook) 5 times, yo and draw through all lps on hook. Fasten off. Fold last 2 rnds to wrong side and sew edge to base of first C border rnd for hem.

Radiant Surprise

The appeal of this pattern comes from
the combination of pastel colors
with dashes of deep rose, dusky blue,
and some unexpected variegated hexagons.

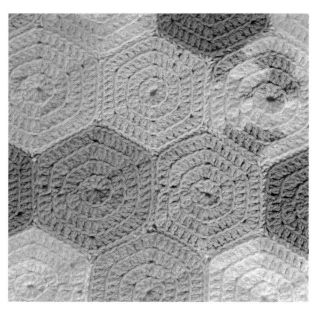

Mary S. Kelly
Washington, D.C.

Mary Kelly is probably the most experienced crocheter of all the prizewinners. She has been at it for seventy-three years! She reminisces with pleasure about her first project, when she was seven. She was invited to join her mother, grandmother, sisters, and aunt at the table where they were busily working with yarns:

"I was given a ball of soft white cotton yarn and a steel hook. With these tools plus hours of patient instructions and many frustrations, I miraculously created a *washcloth.* How proud I was as I finally wrapped it with all its imperfections in tissue paper and ribbon to give to my mother for Christmas."

The thrill of that handmade gift has never left Mary, who over the years has crocheted countless gifts for her children and grandchildren. She plans to give this splendid afghan to her daughter—who still has the first one Mary made over fifty years ago!

SIZE

About 49″ × 64″

MATERIALS

Yarn: Knitting worsted, 60 oz. assorted pastel colors (use scraps if you wish), including 3 oz. baby pastel variegated yarn for border.

Crochet hook: Size F (4.00 mm) or size that gives you correct gauge.

GAUGE

Each hexagon measures 3¾″ across from side to opposite side, about 4″ across from point to opposite point.

STITCHES

Ch, sl st, sc, dc

Degree of difficulty: **

DIRECTIONS

Note: Work all rnds from right side.

Hexagons

Make 228. Starting at center with desired color, ch 5. Join with sl st to form ring.

Rnd 1: Ch 3 (counts as first dc), 11 dc in ring (12 dc, counting ch 3); join with sl st to top of ch 3.

Rnd 2: Ch 3, working in back lp only of sts throughout, work (3 dc in next dc, dc in next dc) 5 times, work 3 dc in last dc; join.

Rnd 3: Ch 3, dc in next dc, * 3 dc in next dc (corner made), dc in next 3 dc; repeat from * around, ending with dc in last dc; join.

Rnd 4: Ch 3, dc in next 2 dc, * 3 dc in next dc (corner made), dc in next 5 dc; repeat from * around, ending with dc in last 2 dc; join. Fasten off.

Assembly

Arranging color as desired, join hexagons in 19 strips of 12 hexagons each, holding hexagons right sides together and sewing through back lps only of corresponding sts along adjoining edges. Following Assembly Diagram, Figure 7, sew strips together to form panel about 48″ × 63″.

Border

Attach variegated yarn to afghan at X. Crochet in back loop of sts for scalloped border: Work (5 sc, 3 dc) around, working 2 sts at each outer corner, skipping 1 st at inner corners, and working 1 st in each remaining edge st, to keep edge of work flat and smooth. Join and fasten off when rnd is completed.

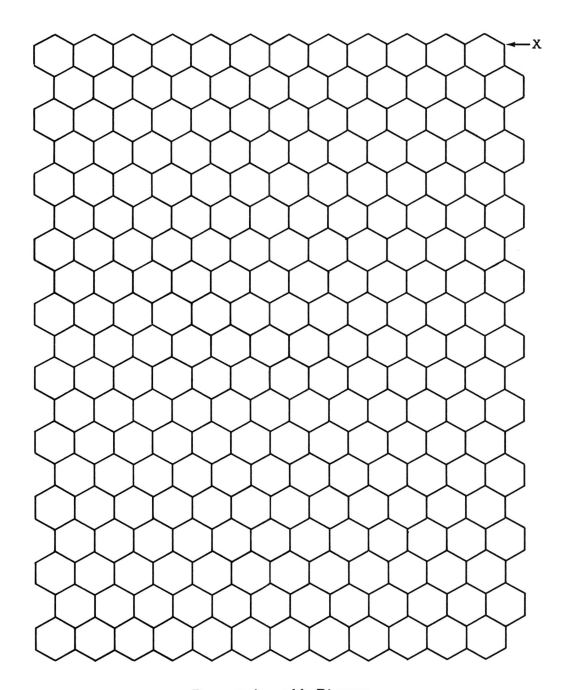

Figure 7. Assembly Diagram

Rainbow Baby Hexagons

These simple hexagons will delight any
enterprising beginner. They make the most of
popular variegated yarn by coordinating
it with solid-color units.

Ruth P. Kaplan-Kramer
Media, Pennsylvania

Psychotherapist Ruth Kaplan-Kramer knows firsthand the therapeutic
qualities of needlework. When she developed medical problems related
to her pregnancy and had to stay in bed for a month, working on her
baby's afghan helped her cope with her anxiety.

Ruth's mother was an occupational therapist and taught her knitting,
crocheting, needlepoint, cross-stitch, and embroidery when she was a
child. Although she has concentrated primarily on making jewelry as a
hobby for the past ten years, Ruth has always had a needlework project
going at the same time.

"Many of my recent jewelry designs have been based on the interplay
of colors of different metals: silver, copper, brass. That interest carried
over into the design of the Rainbow Baby afghan." Each hexagon uses
variegated yarn with a coordinating solid color.

SIZE

Each hexagon measures 4½" across from side to side. To make an afghan of the size you desire, see page 165, Designing on Your Own.

MATERIALS

Yarn: Knitting worsted *for each hexagon:* 9 yd. baby pastel variegated or ombre (color A), 15 yd. coordinating solid color (B). See page 166, for how to estimate amount of yarn needed for an afghan.

Crochet hook: Size F (4.00 mm) or size that gives you correct gauge.

STITCHES

Ch, sl st, dc

Degree of difficulty: *

DIRECTIONS

Note: Work all rnds from right side.

Hexagon

Starting at center with color A, ch 4. Join with sl st to form ring.

Rnd 1: Ch 3 (counts as first dc), dc in ring, ch 1, (2 dc in ring, ch 1) 5 times; join to top of ch 3.

Rnd 2: Ch 4, * work (2 dc, ch 1, 2 dc) in next sp, ch 1; repeat from * around 4 times more, (2 dc, ch 1, 1 dc) in last sp; join to 3rd ch of ch 4.

Rnd 3: Ch 3, dc in next sp, * ch 1, (2 dc, ch 1, 2 dc) in next sp (corner made), ch 1, 2 dc in next sp; repeat from * around, ending with 6th corner, ch 1; join. Fasten off.

Rnd 4: Attach B to any corner sp, ch 3, (dc, ch 1, 2 dc) in same sp, * (ch 1, 2 dc in next sp) twice, ch 1, (2 dc, ch 1, 2 dc) in next corner sp; repeat from * around, ending with 2 dc in last sp, ch 1; join.

Rnd 5: Ch 4, * (2 dc, ch 1, 2 dc) in next corner sp, (ch 1, 2 dc in next sp) 3 times, ch 1; repeat from * around, ending with dc in last sp; join to 3rd ch of ch 4. Fasten off.

Joining

To sew: Pin together edges to be sewn. Thread needle with matching yarn. Sew edges with whipstitch working through one or both loops (as desired) of corresponding stitches along adjoining edges. Weave yarn ends through corresponding stitches along adjoining edges.

To crochet: With matching yarn, slip stitch or single crochet through corresponding stitches along adjoining edges.

Blue Snowflakes

For warmth and beauty,
it's hard to beat this
reversible piggyback square.

M. Kathleen Eckman
Maupin, Oregon

This grandmother of thirteen claims to have made several hundred afghans, sweaters, and bedspreads in her long love affair with crocheting. "You might say I'm hooked," she quips.

She taught herself how to crochet and has taught many others besides. Her husband loves to watch TV, so while keeping him company, Kathleen, who is a retired secretary, knits and crochets. She has produced many of her afghans during football season. When asked how she can crochet and follow the game, she says: "Oh, I just listen and when the crowd roars, I watch the instant replays."

Her contest entry, a cozy stadium blanket, was designed for her grandniece, who is now in college. Since her niece loves blue, Kathleen made the afghan blue on blue and used four different squares, including double squares made by overlapping a small square on a larger one. It took her a couple of weeks to complete, including the time she spent ripping in order to get the overlays the right size.

SIZE
About 56″ square for complete afghan.

MATERIALS
Yarn: Knitting worsted; *for complete prize-winning afghan:* 28 oz. each royal blue (color A) and light blue (B). See individual square directions for yarn amounts if you are designing your own afghan.

Crochet hook: Size J (6.00 mm) or size that gives you correct gauge.

GAUGE
Large squares measure 7¾″ across; small squares measure 4¼″ across.

STITCHES
Ch, sl st, dc, tr, d tr, tr tr

Degree of difficulty: ***

DIRECTIONS FOR COMPLETE AFGHAN
Following directions for squares below, make 12 Large Blue-on-Blue Squares, 12 Small Blue-on-Blue Squares, 13 Large Blue-on-Blue Overlaid Squares and 32 Small Blue-on-Blue Overlaid Squares.

Large Blue-on-Blue Square
MATERIALS FOR INDIVIDUAL SQUARE

Yarn: Knitting worsted; *for each square:* 7½ yd. royal blue (color A), 37 yd. light blue (B). See page 166 for how to estimate yarn amounts for an afghan.

DIRECTIONS FOR EACH SQUARE
Starting at center with color B, ch 5. Join with sl st to form ring.

Rnd 1 (wrong side): Ch 3 (counts as first dc), work 2 dc in ring, work (ch 2, 3 dc in ring) 3 times, ch 2; join with sl st in top of ch 3.

Rnd 2: Ch 3, turn work, (2 dc, ch 2, 3 dc) in next ch-2 sp (first corner made), * ch 1, work (3 dc, ch 2, 3 dc) in next corner ch-2 sp (another corner made); repeat from * around, ending ch 1; join to top of ch 3. Fasten off B; attach A to corner sp.

Rnd 3: Without turning work, ch 3, (2 dc, ch 2, 3 dc) in corner sp, * ch 1, dc in next sp, work tr tr (see page 163) around post of center dc of 3-dc group of Rnd 1 (directly below same sp), work dc in same sp as last dc, ch 1, work (3 dc, ch 2, 3 dc) in next corner sp; repeat from * around, ending ch 1; join. Fasten off A; turn, attach B to last ch-1 sp before any corner.

Rnd 4: Ch 3, work 2 dc in same ch-1 sp, * ch 1, work corner, (ch 1, work 3 dc in next ch-1 sp) twice; repeat from * around, ending with ch 1; join.

Rnd 5: Ch 3, turn, work 2 dc in next sp, then work (ch 1, 3 dc, ch 2, 3 dc) in each corner sp and (ch 1, 3 dc) in each ch-1 sp around; ending with ch 1; join.

Rnd 6: Ch 3, with same side of work facing you and working in back lps of sts, * dc in each remaining dc and ch to next corner ch-2 lp, 2 dc in first ch, ch 2, 2 dc in next ch; repeat from * around, ending with dc in last st; join. Fasten off.

Small Blue-on-Blue Square
MATERIALS FOR INDIVIDUAL SQUARE
Yarn: Knitting worsted; *for each square:* 7½ yd. royal blue (color A), 6½ yd. light blue (B). See page 166 for how to estimate yarn amounts for an afghan.

DIRECTIONS FOR SQUARE
Work same as for large blue-on-blue flower square until Rnd 3 is completed. Fasten off.

Large Blue-on-Blue Overlaid Square
MATERIALS FOR INDIVIDUAL SQUARE
Yarn: Knitting worsted; *for each square:* 35 yd. royal blue (color A), 23 yd. light blue (B). See page 166 for how to estimate yarn amounts for an afghan.

DIRECTIONS FOR SQUARE
Square is worked in two layers, an overlay section and a background section. The edges of the overlay section are joined to the background as you crochet Rnd 5 of the background.

Overlay
Starting at center with color B, ch 5. Join with sl st to form ring.

Rnd 1 (right side): Ch 3 (counts as first dc), work 2 dc in ring, work (ch 5, 3 dc in ring) 3 times, ch 5; join with sl st in top of ch 3.

Rnd 2: Sl st in top of next dc (center dc of 3-dc group), ch 8, sl st in 3rd ch from hook (picot made), ch 1, tr in same dc, * ch 3, sl st in 2nd ch of next ch-5 lp, ch 13, sl st in 4th ch of same ch-5 lp, ch 3, work (tr, ch 4, sl st in 3rd ch from hook for picot, ch 1, tr) in center dc of next 3-dc group; repeat from * around, ending last repeat with ch 3, sl st in 4th ch of starting ch 8. Fasten off, weaving in cut end. Set piece aside.

Background
Starting at center with color A, ch 5. Join with sl st to form ring.

Rnd 1 (wrong side): Ch 3, work 2 dc in ring, work (ch 2, 3 dc) 3 times, ch 2; join with sl st to top of ch 3.

Rnd 2: Ch 3, turn work, (2 dc, ch 2, 3 dc) in next ch-2 sp (first corner made), * ch 1, work (3 dc, ch 2, 3 dc) in next corner ch-2 sp (another corner made); repeat from * around, ending ch 1, join to top of ch 3.

Rnd 3: Ch 3, turn, 2 dc in next ch-1 sp, * ch 1, work corner in next corner sp, ch 1, 3 dc in next ch-1 sp; repeat from * around, ending with ch 1; join.

Rnd 4: Ch 3, turn, work 2 dc in first ch-1 sp, * ch 1, work corner, (ch 1, work 3 dc in next ch-1 sp) twice; repeat from * around, ending with ch 1; join.

Rnd 5 (joining rnd): Ch 3, turn, hold overlay right side up in front of work with long ch-13 lps at corners and picots at center of each side edge of background square, work dc in ch-1 sp by inserting hook front to back through picot and ch-1 sp (picot caught in base of dc just made), work another dc in same sp (but not through picot), * ch 1, 3 dc in next sp, ch 1, in corner sp work 2 dc, then work next dc inserting hook through ch-13 lp of overlay, then into corner sp to catch lp in st, ch 2, dc catching same overlay lp in st as before, work 2 more regular dc, ch 1, 3 dc in next sp, ch 1 (dc, dc catching picot, dc) in next sp; repeat from * around, ending ch 1; join. Fasten off A; attach B to any dc.

Rnd 6: Ch 3, with same side of work facing you and working in back lps only, * dc in each dc and ch to next corner ch-2 lp, 2 dc in first ch, ch 2, 2 dc in next ch; repeat from

* around, ending with dc in last st; join. Fasten off.

Small Blue-on-Blue Overlaid Square
MATERIALS FOR INDIVIDUAL SQUARE

Yarn: Knitting worsted; *for each square:* 13½ yd. royal blue (color A), 3 yd. light blue (B). See page 166 for how to estimate yarn amounts for an afghan.

DIRECTIONS FOR SQUARE

Overlay
Work same as overlay for large blue-on-blue overlaid square until Rnd 1 is completed. Fasten off.

Background
Work same as background for large blue-on-blue overlaid square until Rnd 2 is completed.

Rnd 3 (joining rnd): Sl st to next corner sp, ch 3, (2 dc, ch 2, 3 dc) in corner sp, holding overlay right side up in front of work with ch-5 lps at center of each side edge of background square, * ch 1, dc in next ch-1 sp, work next dc inserting hook through ch-5 lp of overlay then into same sp on background square to catch lp in st, work another regular dc in same sp (not catching lp), ch 1, work corner in next corner; repeat from * around, ending ch 1; join. Fasten off.

Assembly
Lay out large squares, alternating them to form 5- by 5-square panel with overlaid squares at corners. Sew squares together through back loops.

Panel Border
With right side of work facing you, attach A to lp at any corner of panel.

Rnd 1: Ch 3, 2 dc in corner sp, * ch 1, sk 4 dc, (3 dc in next dc, sk 3 dc) 5 times, d tr in corner lp of square, work tr tr reaching ½" down into joining to work st, d tr in corner lp of next square; repeat from * to next panel corner, work (3 dc, ch 2, 3 dc) in corner sp **; repeat from * to ** around panel, ending with (3 dc, ch 2) in first corner, join to top of ch 3.

Rnd 2: Ch 3, turn work; working corners as before, work 3 dc in each ch-1 sp around; join. Fasten off A; attach B to corner lp.

Rnd 3: With right side of work facing you, working in back loop only, dc in each dc and ch 1 around, working (2 dc in first ch, ch 2, 2 dc in next ch) in each corner ch-2 lp; join.

Rnd 4: On right side, ch 3, dc in each dc, working corners as on last rnd; join. Fasten off.

Outer Border
Sew together Small Overlaid Squares to form 4 strips of 8 squares each. Sew a Small Blue-on-Blue Square to each end of each strip. Sew a strip to each side of afghan, adding one of the remaining 4 small squares at each corner.

Edging
Rnd 1: With right side of work facing you, attach A to corner lp, over same lp work (ch 3, then ch 3 again and sl st in first ch of

these 3 ch for picot, dc, ch 1, then ch 3 and complete picot as before, ch 1, dc, picot, dc—first corner made), * ch 1, (3 dc in next ch-1 sp, ch 1) twice, tr in corner lp of square, d tr into joining, picot, tr in corner lp of next square; repeat from * around, working (dc, picot, dc, ch 1, picot, ch 1, dc, picot, dc) at corners; join to top of first ch-3. Fasten off A; attach B at same place.

Rnd 2: ** Ch 6, sk picot, sl st in next dc and ch-1 of corner lp, ch 6, sk picot, sl st in next ch and dc, ch 6, sk picot, sl st in last dc of corner group, * sl st in next ch, ch 3, (2 dc, picot, dc) in next ch-1 sp, ch 3, sl st in next ch and tr, ch 6, sk next d tr and picot, sl st in tr; repeat from * across to next corner; repeat from ** around; join to base of ch-6. Fasten off.

Lacy Baby

**Light and airy pastel grannies
are just perfect for this dainty
blanket for a newborn babe.**

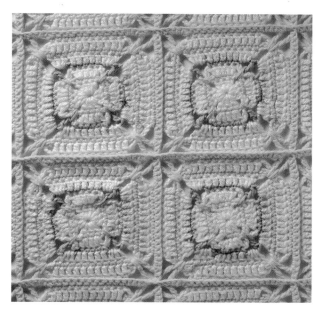

Sue Schult
Cossayuna, New York

Sue Schult has six children, ages two through fourteen, baby-sits for three more, and still has energy left over to crochet, a craft she learned from her mother when she was ten. Sue has already passed down the tradition to her daughter Paula, eleven, who has just finished a vest to enter in the county fair. Tabitha, nine, can crochet a little and the two youngest "only know how to play with my yarn and lose my crochet hook when I'm not looking." Her entire family is very supportive and when "I work on new designs or patterns, they'll tell me if something doesn't look right."

Sue decided to make a baby blanket from granny squares "because I like anything that has to do with babies." The light, open-work design and the gentle ridges formed from crocheting the squares together gives the blanket its special touch. Sue also knits, embroiders, and sews, and often sells items she has made in local boutiques.

SIZE

Each square measures 6¾" across. To make an afghan of the size you desire, see page 165, Designing on Your Own.

MATERIALS

Yarn: Knitting worsted; *for each square:* 18 yd. white (color A), 8 yd. pink (B); 4 yd. each blue (C) and yellow (D). See page 166 for how to estimate amount of yarn needed for an afghan.

Crochet hook: Size I (5.50 mm) or size that gives you correct gauge.

STITCHES

Ch, sl st, sc, dc, tr, long tr (directions given below)

Degree of difficulty: ***

DIRECTIONS

Note: Work all rnds from right side.

Square

Starting at center with color A, ch 4. Join with sl st to form ring.

Rnd 1: Ch 3 (counts as first dc), 2 dc in ring, (ch 3, 3 dc in ring) 3 times, ch 3; join with sl st to top of starting ch 3. Fasten off A; attach B.

Rnd 2: Sc in same place as joining, sc in next 2 dc, ch 4 (corner lp made), work (dc in next 3 dc, ch 4) 3 times; join to first sc. Fasten off B; attach A.

Rnd 3: Ch 3, dc in same place as joining, dc in next sc, 2 dc in next sc, * ch 5 (corner lp made), 2 dc in next sc, dc in next sc, 2

dc in next sc; repeat from * around, ending with ch 5; join to top of ch 3. Fasten off A; attach C.

Rnd 4: Sc in joining; sc in next 4 dc, * ch 3, make long tr at corner as follows: yo twice, reaching hook into corner sp of Rnd 1, draw up long lp, (yo and draw through first 2 lps on hook) 3 times (long tr made enclosing corner lps of Rnds 1, 2, and 3 in base of st), ch 3, sc in next 5 dc; repeat from * around, ending with ch 3; join to first sc. Fasten off C; attach A.

Rnd 5: Ch 3, dc in next 4 sc, * 3 dc over next ch-3 lp, ch 3, 3 dc over next ch-3 lp, dc in next 5 sc; repeat from * around, ending with 3 dc over last lp; join to top of starting ch 3. Fasten off A; attach D.

Rnd 6: Sc in joining, (sc in each dc to next corner, ch 4) 4 times; sc in remaining 3 dc; join to first sc. Fasten off D; attach A.

Rnd 7: Ch 3, (dc in each sc to next corner, ch 6) 4 times; dc in remaining 3 sc; join. Fasten off A; attach B.

Rnd 8: Sc in joining, * sc in each dc to next corner, (ch 3, work long tr as before reaching into corner sp of Rnd 5) twice, ch 3; repeat from * around, ending sc in last 3 dc. Fasten off.

Joining

Holding *wrong* sides of squares together and crocheting sc with B on right side of work, working through both lps of corresponding sts along adjoining edges.

Quilt Block Patterns

The dramatically beautiful designs in this section have been derived and adapted from quilts, then translated into works of art made of granny squares by our skilled crocheters. The secret to success is often subtle use of color and careful organization of the squares to create an exciting optical illusion.

Dusk and Dew

The depth and complexity created by
a stunning combination of colors
make this design a second-prize winner.

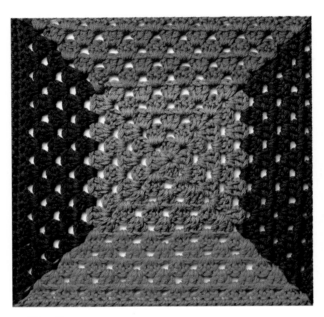

Carole Jean Beck
Huntington Beach, California

Carole supports the three of her four sons who remain at home by raising other folks' kids: She's a professional baby-sitter. So, while rocking and watching, she often crochets, and has made some two hundred afghans.

In fact, she crocheted one for a contest a few years back, after studying quilt books and checking out the fashion colors on display in her local mall. But she decided those colors didn't look right, gave it away, and crocheted another, in a different palette—too late for that contest! A year later, a friend saw it and decided to enter it in this contest, and her dusky country-landscape colors made Carole a winner.

Carole, a self-taught crocheter, used the prize for a camping vacation. "We all love to camp." She is a walker—three to four miles each morning—and she likes to learn new skills. She spent eight years studying guitar, banjo, and mandolin, and plans to return "yet again" to college to learn architectural drafting.

SIZE

About 57" × 79"

MATERIALS

Yarn: Knitting worsted, 19 oz. gray (color A); 12½ oz. each dark blue (B), light blue (C), dark green (D), and purple (E)

Crochet hook: Size I (5.50 mm) or size that gives you correct gauge.

GAUGE

Each square measures 11" across.

STITCHES

Ch, sl st, sc, dc

Degree of difficulty: ***

DIRECTIONS

Note: Turn work at end of each rnd on squares.

Mitered Squares

Make 35. With color A, ch 4. Join with sl st to form ring.

Rnd 1 (right side): Ch 3 (counts as first dc), 2 dc in ring, ch 1, (3 dc in ring, ch 1) 3 times; join to top of ch 3, turn.

Rnd 2: Sl st in first ch-1 sp, ch 3, work 2 dc in same sp, * work (3 dc, ch 1, 3 dc) in next ch-1 sp (corner made); repeat from * twice, 3 dc in first sp, ch 1; join to top of ch 3, turn.

Rnd 3: Sl st in corner sp, ch 3, work 2 dc in same sp, * 3 dc in next sp between 3-dc groups, work corner as before in corner sp; repeat from * twice, 3 dc in next sp between groups, 3 dc in first corner sp, ch 1; join, turn.

Rnd 4: Sl st in first sp, ch 3, 2 dc in same sp, * work 3 dc in each sp between 3-dc groups to next corner, work corner in cor-ner sp; repeat from * around, ending with 3 dc in first corner sp, ch 1; join, turn.

Rnd 5: Repeat Rnd 4, having 1 more 3-dc group each side than on previous rnd. Fasten off. Turn.

Rnd 6: Join B to ch of first corner, * work as before to next corner, work 3 dc in cor-ner sp, drop B; join C and ch 1, work 3 dc in same sp to complete corner, work to next corner, work 3 dc; change to D and work to next corner, work 3 dc; change to E and work to first corner, work 3 dc in first cor-ner, ch 1; join, turn.

Rnds 7 through 10: Continue working as before, adding a 3-dc group to each side on each rnd and working colors as established, changing colors at corners as follows: with old color work 3 dc in corner sp, drop old color and loop from hook, with new color draw up lp in corner sp and ch 3 (counts as first dc), drop lp from hook, insert hook through old color lp and draw new lp through, with new color ch 1, 2 dc in same sp to complete corner.

Rnd 11: Sl st in corner sp, * sc in corner sp, sc in each dc of same color to next cor-ner, draw up lp in corner sp; fasten off old color, with next color, yo and draw through lps on hook to complete last sc of old color, work with new color and repeat from * around, ending with sc in first corner with B; join to first E sc. Fasten off.

Assembly

Holding squares right side together with B edge of one square matching D edge of next square and using B yarn, join squares with sc to form 7 strips of 5 squares each. Right sides together, with C edge of one strip matching E edge of next strip and using C yarn, join strips with sc to form afghan 5 squares by 7 squares.

Border

Note: Use larger hook if needed to keep border flat. With right side of work facing you, join A to any corner of afghan.

Rnd 1: Sc in corner, work (ch 1, sk 1 sc, sc in next sc) around afghan, working (sc, ch 1, sc) at corners; join to first sc.

Rnd 2: Sl st in first sp, sc in same sp, work (ch 1, sc in next sp) around, working (sc, ch 1, sc) in each corner sp; join to first sc.

Rnds 3 and 4: Repeat Rnd 2 twice more. Fasten off.

Sierra Pinwheels

This magnificent Sierra pattern uses
seven different colors set off by
striped scalloped borders and
earned its designer first prize.

Rosalie DeVries
Plattsburgh, New York

Our first-prize winner, Rosalie, has been crocheting for twenty-five
years and regularly designs her own patterns. Her grandmother was her
teacher and her inspiration. "I used to watch her crochet and she would
give me a hook and a scrap of yarn and I would make chains." An accomplished all-around craftswoman, this grandmother of three also enjoys knitting, sewing, woodworking, and baking. As a collector of old
needlework books and magazines, Rosalie always has a supply of designs and patterns to suggest ideas for her own work.

The inspiration for the quilt shown here was the sawtoothed ridges of
the Sierra mountains. The pinwheel units are worked into the side of the
stitch so they fall sideways in points, or mountain peaks. Dusty rose,
pink, aqua, bright yellow, and burnt orange suggest the radiant colors of
the far-off mountains.

SIZE

About 49" × 65"

MATERIALS

Yarn: Knitting worsted, 18 oz. teal (color A), 16 oz. dusty rose (B), 12 oz. bright rose (C), 10 oz. pink (D), 6 oz. aqua (E), 4 oz. bright yellow (F), and 1 oz. burnt orange (G).

Crochet hook: Size F (4.00 mm) or size that gives you correct gauge.

GAUGE

Each square measures 7¼" across.

STITCHES

Ch, sl st, sc, hdc, dc, tr

Degree of difficulty: ***

DIRECTIONS

Note: To change colors, fasten off at the end of each rnd. To begin rnd with new color, make slip knot (beginning loop) on hook and work first st of rnd in usual manner. Conceal yarn ends in work.

Work all rnds from right side.

Squares

Make 48. Starting at center with color G, ch 4. Join with sl st to form ring.

Rnd 1: (Sc in ring, ch 5, sl st in 5th ch from hook) 6 times (6 lps made); join to first sc.

Rnd 2: With F, sc in any sc between lps, ch 3, work 3 dc back into side of last sc made (sawtooth point made), * holding lp forward out of way, sc into next sc, ch 3, work 3 dc back into side of last sc (another point made); repeat from * 4 times more (6 points made); join to first sc.

Rnd 3: With A, work 2 sc in top of any point (at top of ch 3), work 3 dc in center ch of next Rnd 1 lp, * work 2 sc in top of next point, 3 dc in center ch of next Rnd 1 lp; repeat from * 4 times more; join to first sc.

Rnd 4: With B, make point as before in first sc, make point in next dc, * make point in next sc, make point in next dc; repeat from * around (12 points made); join.

Rnd 5: With E, 2 sc in top of any point, 3 dc in next sc, * work 2 sc in top of next point, 3 dc in next sc; repeat from * around; join.

Rnd 6: With A, make point in first sc, * sk 2 sts, make point in next st; repeat from * around (20 points); join.

Rnd 7: With C, * (sc in top of next point, 3 dc in next sc) 4 times, 2 sc in top of next point, 3 dc in next sc; repeat from * around; join.

Rnd 8: With D, work 5 tr in first sc (corner made), * tr in next 2 sts, dc in next 3 sts, hdc in next 3 sts, sc in next 4 sts, hdc in next 3 sts, dc in next 3 sts, tr in next 2 sts, 5 tr in next st (another corner made); repeat from * around to first corner, ending with tr in last 2 sts; join to first tr.

Rnd 9: With B, * work 5 dc in center st of corner 5-tr group, dc in next 3 sts, hdc in next 3 sts, sc in next 12 sts, hdc in next 3 sts, dc in next 3 sts; repeat from * around; join. Fasten off.

Assembly

Lay out squares to form a panel 6 squares by 8 squares. Follow Assembly Diagram, Figure 8, to determine color (A or C) with which to work each square's joining border.

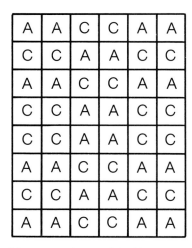

A	A	C	C	A	A
C	C	A	A	C	C
A	A	C	C	A	A
C	C	A	A	C	C
C	C	A	A	C	C
A	A	C	C	A	A
C	C	A	A	C	C
A	A	C	C	A	A

Figure 8. Assembly Diagram

Joining border: *First (corner) square:*
With right side of work facing you, using A,
* sc in 4th dc of corner 5-dc group, work
(ch 3, sk 2 sts, sc in next sc) 9 times, ending in 2nd dc of next corner group, ch 7 for
corner; repeat from * around; join. Fasten
off. *Second square:* Work first 3 sides as
for first square to corner, ch 3, holding
squares wrong sides together, sc in center
ch of corner lp on adjoining first square, ch
3, back on 2nd square sk 2 sts, sc in next st
(corner joining made), * (ch 1, sc in center

ch of next ch-3 lp on adjoining first square,
ch 1, sk 2 sts on 2nd square, sc in next st);
repeat from * to next corner, work another
corner joining as before; join to first sc of
2nd square. Continue in this manner, working joining border around each square and
attaching each adjoining side as you add
squares to form 6-by-8 square panel.

Border

Rnd 1: With B, sc in 5th ch of corner lp
of first corner square, ch 3, dc into sc just
made (scallop made), * working along afghan edge, (sc in center ch of next lp, ch 3,
dc into sc just made—another scallop made)
to next afghan corner, work scallop in 3rd
ch of corner lp, work another scallop in 5th
ch of same corner lp (corner scallop made);
repeat from * around, ending with scallop in
3rd ch of last corner lp; join to first sc.

Rnd 2: With A, sc into 3rd ch of lp at top
of corner scallop and complete scallop as
before, * work scallop in center of next scallop lp; repeat from * around working into
first and 3rd ch of scallop at each corner;
join.

Rnd 3: With C, repeat Rnd 2.

Amish Tumbling Blocks

The richness and arrangement of colors turn this traditional design into a contemporary treasure.

Katherine Eng
San Francisco, California

This talented needleworker won second prize in an earlier *Woman's Day* afghan contest. An accomplished quilter, Katherine had begun at that time to translate quilt designs into crochet projects. She spent a year working on patterns, charts, and various techniques. One of her most unusual contributions is the method used here to connect the units as they are crocheted, so they don't have to be sewn together later.

"The baby block design fascinated me because of the way the pattern tricks the eye. At first you see ribbons or diamonds, then stars or blocks." Rather than use intricate stitches, Katherine concentrated on putting together vibrant Amish colors—dark rose, bright cerise, dark blue-green, violet—and carefully arranging the squares for the final dazzling effect.

A former ballet dancer who now teaches dance in her daughter's school, Katherine has begun to turn her love of needlework into a profession. She has recently done a design project for a clothing manufacturer and looks forward to a whole new career.

SIZE

About 50″ × 56″

MATERIALS

Yarn: Knitting worsted, 24 oz. dark rose (color A), 20 oz. bright cerise (B), 16 oz. dark blue-green (C), 8 oz. violet (D).

Crochet hook: Size G (4.50 mm) or size that gives you correct gauge.

GAUGE

4 sc = 1″

STITCHES

Ch, sl st, sc, dc

Degree of difficulty: ****

DIRECTIONS

Note: Center panel of afghan is crocheted in one piece, made by working diamond shapes to form two-colored zigzag strips alternated with diamond fill-in strips, joined as you work.

First Strip (zigzag strip)

First diamond: Ch 10 with color C. **Row 1 (right side):** Sc in 2nd ch from hook, sc in each remaining ch (9 sc); ch 1, turn. Mark right side of work with safety pin. **Row 2:** Work 2 sc in first sc (inc made), sc in each sc to last 2 sc, draw up lp in each of last 2 sc, yo and draw through all 3 lps on hook (dec made); ch 1, turn. Maintain 9 sc on each row. **Row 3:** Work dec as before on first 2 sc, sc in each sc to last sc, work inc as before (9 sc); ch 1, turn. Side edges of work slant. Repeat Rows 2 and 3 three times more. Fasten off C.

Second diamond: **Row 1:** With right side of work facing you and using A, sc in each sc across; ch 1, turn. **Row 2:** Dec, sc to last sc, inc; ch 1, turn. **Row 3:** Inc, sc to last 2 sc, dec; ch 1, turn. Repeat last 2 rows 3 times more. Fasten off A.

Third diamond: **Row 1:** With right side of work facing you and using C, sc in each sc across; ch 1, turn. Starting with Row 2 of first diamond, continue working diamonds in zigzag strip, alternating A and C until 18 diamonds are completed (see Figure 9A). Fasten off.

Second Strip (fill-in diamond strip)

First diamond: **Row 1:** With right side of work facing you, attach B to lower right corner of first strip (at X on Figure 9A) and work 9 sc along edge from X to Y; sl st in first row of second diamond, then sl st in 2nd row of second diamond to join edges; ch 1, turn. **Row 2:** Inc in first sc, sc to last 2 sc, dec; ch 1, turn. **Row 3:** Dec, sc to last sc, inc; sl st in next 2 rows to join to previous strip; ch 1, turn. Repeat last 2 rows 3 times more, ending at Z. Do not fasten off.

Second diamond: Continuing with B, start at Z and work next diamond along 3rd diamond edge of previous strip, joining to 4th diamond edge. Continue along strip in this manner until 9 diamonds are completed on second strip. Fasten off.

Third Strip (zigzag strip)

First diamond: Attach A to lower point of first diamond of previous strip; ch 10. **Row 1 (right side):** Sc in 2nd and each remaining ch across (9 sc); sl st in first 2 rows of diamond to join; ch 1, turn. **Row 2:** Dec, sc to last sc, inc; ch 1, turn. **Row 3:** Inc, sc to last 2 sc, dec; sl st in next 2 rows to join; ch 1, turn. Repeat last 2 rows 3 times more. Fasten off A.

Second diamond: Attach C to upper right corner of previous diamond (W on Figure 9B). *Row 1 (right side):* Sc in each sc across; sl st in next 2 rows to join; ch 1, turn. *Row 2:* Inc, sc to last 2 sc, dec; ch 1, turn. *Row 3:* Dec, sc to last sc, inc; sl st in next 2 rows to join; ch 1, turn. Repeat last 2 rows 3 times more. Fasten off C.

Third diamond: On right of work, attach A to upper right corner of previous diamond. *Row 1:* Sc in each sc across; sl st in next 2 sts to join. Complete as for first diamond. Continue working strip alternating C and A to end.

Fourth Strip (fill-in diamond strip)
Attach B to lower right corner at beg of previous strip (V on Figure 9B).

First fill-in triangle (triangle at starting edge): With B, ch 2. *Row 1 (right side):* Sc in 2nd ch from hook, sl st in first 2 rows of previous strip to join; ch 1, turn. *Row 2:* 2 sc in sc; ch 1, turn. *Row 3:* Sc in first sc, inc in last sc (3 sc); sl st in 2 rows to join; ch 1, turn. *Row 4:* Inc, sc to end; ch 1, turn. *Row 5:* Sc to last sc, inc; sl st in next 2 rows to join; ch 1, turn. Repeat these last 2 rows twice more; ch 1, do not turn.

Next diamond: *Row 1:* Work 9 sc along edge of next diamond of previous strip; sl st in next 2 rows to join; ch 1, turn. Now continue working fill-in diamond strip as for second strip, ending with 8th complete diamond.

Last fill-in triangle (at top edge): *Row 1:* Continuing with B, work 9 sc across edge of last diamond on previous strip to top; ch 1, turn. *Row 2:* Sc to last 2 sc, dec; ch 1,

turn. *Row 3:* Dec, sc to end; ch 1, turn. Repeat last 2 rows 3 times (1 sc remaining). Fasten off.

Fifth Strip (zigzag strip)
Attach C to lower right point of triangle on previous row; ch 10. Complete strip in same manner as before, alternating C and A diamonds and joining to previous strip.

Continue working zigzag and fill-in diamond strips as before until piece measures about 46″ from beg, ending with 14th zigzag strip.

Fill-in End Strips
With right side of work facing you, attach B to right-hand corner of one jagged edge.

Fill-in triangle (at right-hand edge): *Row 1:* Ch 2, sc in 2nd ch from hook, sl st in first 2 rows along jagged edge to join; ch 1, turn. *Row 2:* 2 sc in sc (inc made); ch 1, turn. *Row 3:* Sc in first sc, inc in last sc (3 sc); sl st in next 2 rows to join; ch 1, turn. *Row 4:* Inc, sc to end; ch 1, turn. *Row 5:* Sc to last sc, inc; sl st to join; ch 1, turn. *Row 6:* Inc, sc in next sc, dec, sk last sc; ch 1, turn. *Row 7:* Dec, sc in next sc, inc; sl st to join; ch 1, turn. *Row 8:* Inc, dec, sk last sc; ch 1, turn. *Row 9:* Sl st in first sc, dec; join to last row of first diamond; ch 1, do not turn.

Fill-in half-diamond: *Row 1:* Work 9 sc along edge of next diamond along jagged edge; sl st in 2 rows of next diamond to join; ch 1, turn. *Row 2:* Inc, sc to last 3 sc, dec, sk last sc; ch 1, turn. *Row 3:* Dec, sc to last sc, inc, sl st to join; ch 1, turn. *Rows 4 and 5:* Repeat Rows 2 and 3 once more. *Row 6:* Inc, sc to last 4 sc, dec, sk last 2 sc (5 sc); ch 1, turn. *Row 7:* Sl st in first 2 sc, ch 1, dec in next 2 sc, inc (3 sc); sl st to join; ch 1, turn. *Row 8:* Dec 1, sk 1; ch 1, turn. *Row 9:* Sc in last sc; sl st to point of next diamond.

Work in this manner across jagged edge, filling in small space at end as follows:

Fill-in triangle (at left-hand edge): *Row 1:* Work 9 sc in edge of last diamond; ch 1, turn. *Row 2:* Dec, sc to last 2 sc, dec; ch 1, turn. *Rows 3 and 4:* Repeat Row 2 twice more. *Row 5:* Dec, sc in last sc; ch 1, turn. *Row 6:* Dec. Fasten off.

Turn afghan and work remaining jagged edge to correspond.

Border

Rnd 1: With right side of work facing you, attach D to edge just after any corner and sc around edge, working 17 sc across half-diamonds, 9 sc across diamonds and triangle edges, and 3 sc at each corner; join with sl st to first sc; ch 1, turn.

Rnd 2: Work (sc in next sc, ch 1, sk 1 sc) around, working 3 sc in center sc at each corner; join to first sc; ch 1, turn.

Rnd 3: Sc in first ch-1 sp, then sc in each sc and ch-1 sp, working 3 sc in center sc at each corner; join; ch 1, turn.

Rnds 4 through 7: Repeat Rnds 2 and 3 twice more. Fasten off D. On wrong side of work, attach B to sc just after any corner.

Rnd 8 (wrong side): Repeat Rnd 2, ending ch 3, turn.

Rnd 9: Dc in each sc and sp around, working 3 dc in center sc at corners; join to top of ch-3; ch 1, turn.

Rnd 10: Work (sc in next dc, ch 1, sk 1 dc) around, working (sc, ch 1, sc) at corners; join. Fasten off B. On right side of work, attach A to any ch-1 sp and ch 3.

Rnd 11: Dc in same sp, work 2 dc in each remaining sp around, working (2 dc, ch 2, 2 dc) in each corner sp; join; ch 1, turn.

Rnd 12: Sc in first sp between 2-dc groups, work (ch 1, sc in next sp between dc groups) around, working (sc, ch 3, sc) over each corner lp; ch 1, join; ch 3, turn.

Rnds 13 and 14: Repeat Rnds 11 and 12.

Rnd 15: Work as for Rnd 11, but work (ch 1, 2 dc, ch 2, 2 dc, ch 1) at each corner.

Rnd 16: Work as for Rnd 12, but work (sc in first ch-1 sp at corner, sc in 2 dc, 3 sc over corner lp, sc in 2 dc, sc in last ch-1 sp at corner) at each corner.

Rnd 17 (shell rnd): Sc in first sp, * 3 dc in next sp (shell made), sc in next sp; repeat from * around to first sc at next corner, sc in next sc, 3-dc shell in next sc, sc in next sc, shell in next sc (center of corner), sc in next sc, shell in next sc, sc in next sc of corner; repeat from * around to last sp; join to first sc; ch 1, turn.

Rnd 18 (picot rnd): * Sl st in center dc of next shell, ch 2, sl st in same dc (picot made), ch 1, sl st in next sc, ch 1; repeat from * around, working ch 3 for picots in corner shells; join to first st. Fasten off.

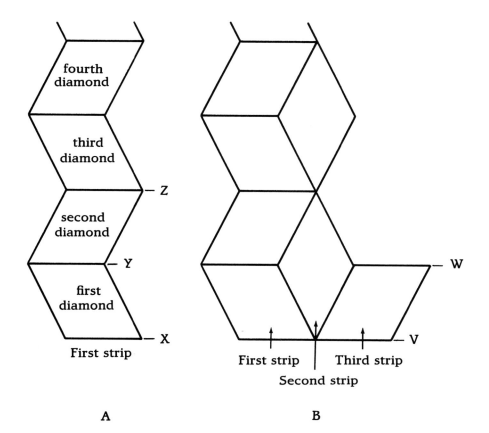

Figure 9.

Cottage Blues

This blue-and-white beauty
with its charming provincial feeling
is as fresh as a day in the country.

Beulah Jo Hamman
Festus, Missouri

Like many of the prizewinning crocheters, Beulah is also proficient in other needlework, particularly sewing and knitting. But crocheting is her favorite. "I am always working on at least one thing," she says, which she enjoys giving to someone she loves. The country-crisp afghan shown here was made for her son-in-law, who is very fond of blue.

The idea for this work came from a star quilt pattern Beulah found in a magazine. In adapting it to granny squares, Beulah uses color to trick the eye. Solid-color squares are combined with two-color squares in white and blue. By carefully orchestrating the arrangement of the squares, Beulah creates the illusion of dancing forms and shapes.

SIZE
About 40½" × 56½"

MATERIALS
Yarn: Knitting worsted, 25 oz. light blue (color A), 25 oz. white (B), 7 oz. royal blue (C).

Crochet hook: Size G (4.50 mm) or size that gives you correct gauge.

GAUGE
Each square measures 4" across.

STITCHES
Ch, sl st, sc, dc

Degree of difficulty: *

DIRECTIONS
Note: Afghan is made of three types of squares: solid light blue, white and light blue, white and royal blue. The squares are turned as needed to form patchwork design shown.

Work all rnds from right side.

Solid-Color Squares
Make 24 (these are indicated as square 1 on Assembly Diagram). Starting at center with color A, ch 4. Join with sl st to form ring.

Rnd 1: Ch 4 (counts as first dc and corner sp), work (3 dc in ring, ch 1) 3 times, 2 dc in ring; join with sl st to 3rd ch of ch 4 to complete first corner.

Rnd 2: Sl st in corner sp, ch 4, work 3 dc in same corner sp, * ch 1, (3 dc, ch 1, 3 dc) in next corner sp; repeat from * twice more, ch 1, 2 dc in first corner sp; join to 3rd ch of ch 4.

Rnd 3: Sl st in corner sp, ch 4, 3 dc in same sp, * ch 1, 3 dc in next ch-1 sp, ch 1, (3 dc, ch 1, 3 dc) in next corner sp; repeat from * around, ending with 2 dc in first corner sp; join as before.

Rnd 4: Sl st in corner sp, ch 4, 3 dc in same sp, * ch 1, (3 dc in next ch-1 sp, ch 1) twice, (3 dc, ch 1, 3 dc) in next corner sp; repeat from * around, ending with 2 dc in first corner sp; join. Fasten off.

Two-Color Squares
Make 24 with colors B and C (square 3 on Assembly Diagram), 92 with colors A and B (square 2 on Assembly Diagram).

Note: To change colors, work with old color until last 2 lps of last st remain on hook, then with new color, yo and draw through last 2 lps to complete st, continue with new color. Throughout, carry color not in use behind top edge of work, concealing it in sts as you crochet. A bit of carried yarn will show between dc groups on wrong side of work.

Starting at center with B, ch 4. Join with sl st to form ring.

Rnd 1: Ch 4, 3 dc in ring, changing to blue (A or C) on last st, ch 1, carrying B work (3 dc, ch 1, 3 dc) in ring, changing to B on last st, ch 1, work 2 dc in ring; join with sl st to 3rd ch of ch 4.

Rnd 2: Sl st in corner sp, ch 4, 3 dc in same sp, ch 1, 3 dc in next sp, changing to blue, ch 1, 3 dc in same sp (2nd corner made), ch 1, (3 dc, ch 1, 3 dc) in next corner sp, ch 1, work 3 dc in next corner sp, changing to B, ch 1, work 3 dc in same corner sp (4th corner made), ch 1, 2 dc in first corner sp; join to 3rd ch of ch 4. Complete as for Rnds 3 and 4 of solid-color square, changing colors at 2nd and 4th corners as before. Fasten off.

Assembly

Following Assembly Diagram, Figure 10, for placement, sew squares together through back lps of corresponding sts along square edges.

Border

With C, crochet a row of sc all around afghan, working 3 sc at each corner.

MORE PATCHWORK

Two-color squares, worked in any two colors, can be adapted to many different patchwork designs (see Figures 11A, B, and C for some suggestions). To design your own, block out pattern on graph paper or cut squares and triangles from construction paper, arranging and shifting them around until you find a pleasing pattern.

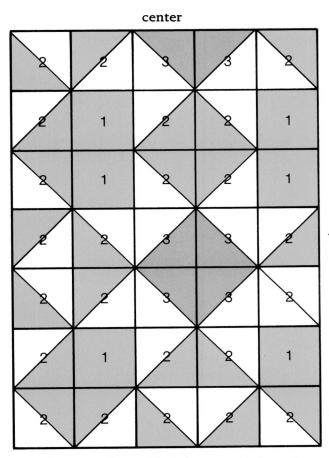

center

Figure 10. Assembly Diagram (¼ shown)

1 = solid-color square
2 = two-color square with A and B
3 = two-color square with B and C

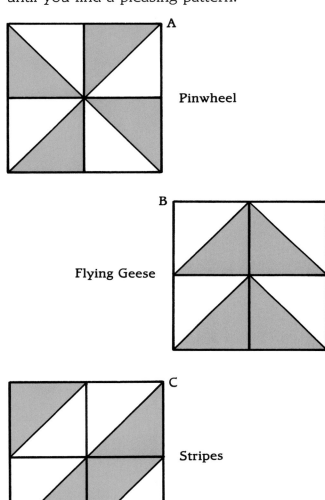

A Pinwheel

B Flying Geese

C Stripes

Figure 11.

79

Log Cabin Rainbow

**The slash of black that frames the glorious colors
in this easy-to-do design gives this
favorite old pattern a sleek contemporary look.**

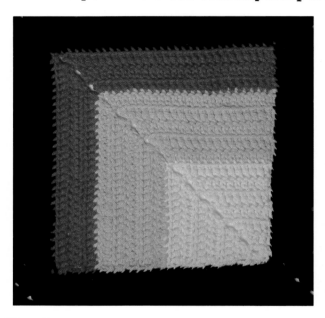

Helen M. Noteboom
Richland, Michigan

Helen has been crocheting sweaters, mittens, hats, scarves, slippers, rugs, and afghans for her two stepchildren and five grandchildren for many years. She finds crocheting very restful and likes to work on projects in the evening while watching TV. Now retired, after twenty-two years teaching elementary school, she has more time to devote to crocheting and to gardening, her other favorite hobby. She has been a member of her garden club for twenty-four years and its treasurer for twelve. Seventy-nine years old, and married for forty-six years, Helen finds lots of things grow better with age.

Helen plans to give this resplendent bed throw to her daughter, since it was she who encouraged her to enter the contest. It was made with scraps of yarn left over from the fifteen other afghans Helen had made. So she decided to use rainbow colors in a unique pattern. With light colors shading into dark, and the unit defined by a striking black border, this adaptation of the Log Cabin design gains depth and complexity.

SIZE

About 56″ × 74″

MATERIALS

Yarn: Knitting worsted, 24 oz. black (MC); 3 shades each of blue, green, yellow, orange, pink/red, purple: 2 oz. each light shade, 3½ oz. each medium shade, 3 oz. each dark shade.

Crochet hook: Size G (4.50 mm) or size that gives you correct gauge.

GAUGE

Each square measures 9″ across.

STITCHES

Ch, sl st, dc

Degree of difficulty: *

DIRECTIONS

Note: To change color at end of row, work until 2 lps of last st remain; cut off old color and tie on new; with new color, yo and draw through both lps to complete st; continue with new color.

Squares

Make 8 squares with each of six different color families. Starting at lower right corner of square with light shade, ch 4.

Row 1 (right side): Work (dc, ch 3, 2 dc) in 4th ch from hook; ch 3, turn.

Row 2: Working in back lp only of sts from now on, sk first dc, dc in next dc, 2 dc in next ch, ch 3 (corner lp made), sk center ch, 2 dc in next ch, dc in next dc, dc in top of ch-3; ch 3 (counts as first dc on next row), turn.

Row 3: Sk first dc, dc in each dc to corner lp, 2 dc in first ch, ch 3, sk center ch, 2 dc in next ch (corner made), dc in each dc to end; ch 3, turn.

Rows 4 through 7: Repeat Row 3, changing to medium shade on last row.

Rows 8 through 12: With medium shade, repeat Row 3, changing to darkest shade on last row.

Rows 13 through 15: With darkest shade, repeat Row 3, changing to MC on last row.

Rows 16 through 18: With MC, repeat Row 3. Fasten off.

Assembly

Following Assembly Diagram, Figure 12, for placement, and having colored corner at lower right for all squares, sew square edges neatly together.

Border

Work border along the two colored edges (lower and right side of afghan) only. Attach MC to lower left corner of afghan (X on diagram).

Row 1: Ch 3 and dc along afghan edge, spacing dc to keep edges smooth and flat (about 35 dc on each square) to corner (Y on diagram), work 4 dc at corner, then work dc to next corner (Z on diagram); ch 3, turn.

Rows 2 and 3: Work 2 more rows of dc in back lp only, working 4 dc at corner. Fasten off.

1	6	5	4	3	2	Z
6	5	4	3	2	1	
5	4	3	2	1	6	
4	3	2	1	6	5	
3	2	1	6	5	4	
2	1	6	5	4	3	
1	6	5	4	3	2	
6	5	4	3	2	1	

X   Y

Color Key

1   Blue shades
2   Green shades
3   Yellow shades
4   Orange shades
5   Pink/red shades
6   Purple shades

Figure 12. Assembly Diagram

Windmill Squares

Propeller-shaped units, like the arms of a windmill,
and a unique palette of dazzling color
give this design the quality of a contemporary painting.

Shirleen M. Poirier
Palm Bay, Florida

The exquisite combination of unexpected colors—mint green, amethyst, berry, violet, and robin's egg blue—that makes this granny so attractive was no accident. Shirleen is a painter who has always been entranced by color. She has studied art at the University of New Mexico, oil painting at the College of Anchorage, Alaska, and watercolors in Maine.

"Color is my source of inspiration," she explains. "I love to play colors against each other to see what effects can be achieved. By choosing the colors I did, and creating interlocking squares, diamonds, and rectangles, the eye does not focus on the square itself but on the interaction of colors."

Shirleen taught herself to crochet many years ago and found it so relaxing that she uses this art to rest from her painting. She has been creating her own designs for only a few years and is gratified that this is her third design to be published.

SIZE

Each square measures 14″ across. To make an afghan of the size you desire, see page 165, Designing on Your Own.

MATERIALS

Yarn: Knitting worsted; *for each square:* 73 yd. white (color A), 11 yd. each dark green (B), magenta (C), royal blue (D), purple (E), 30 yd. each mint green (F), pink (G), light blue (H), lavender (I). See page 166, for how to estimate amount of yarn needed for an afghan.

Crochet hook: Size G (4.50 mm) or size that gives you correct gauge.

STITCHES

Ch, sl st, sc, dc, tr

Degree of difficulty: ***

DIRECTIONS

Note: Center of square is worked in pieces: a small center block and 4 triangles to form frame for block. Pieces are joined, then outer rnds are worked. *To change colors within rnd,* work to last 2 lps of last old color st; cut old color, attach new color, and complete st. Hide ends in work.

Work all rnds from right side.

Small Center Block

Starting at center with color A, ch 4. Join with sl st to form ring.

Rnd 1: Ch 3 (counts as first dc), work 2 dc in ring, ch 2, (3 dc in ring, ch 2) 3 times more; join to top of ch 3. Fasten off.

Rnd 2: Join B to any ch-2 sp, (ch 3, 2 dc, ch 2, 3 dc) in same sp (first corner made), changing to C in last st; with C, work (3 dc, ch 2, 3 dc) in next sp (another corner

made); with D, work corner in next sp; with E, work corner; join.

Rnd 3: Join B in B corner sp, work first corner as before, * with A, 3 dc in next sp between 3-dc groups; matching corner colors, work next corner; repeat from * around, ending with 3 A dc in last sp; join. Fasten off.

Rnd 4: Join A to any corner sp, work first corner, * 3 dc in each sp to next corner, work corner in next corner sp; repeat from * around, ending 3 dc in last sp; join.

Rnd 5: Sl st to next corner lp, then work as for Rnd 4. Fasten off.

Frame

Triangle: With B, ch 4. *Row 1:* Work (2 dc, ch 2, 3 dc) in 4th ch from hook; ch 3, turn. *Row 2:* Work 2 dc in first dc, work (3 dc, ch 2, 3 dc) in ch-2 sp (corner made), 3 dc in top of ch 3; ch 3, turn. *Row 3:* Work 2 dc in first dc, 3 dc in next sp between 3-dc groups, work corner in corner sp, 3 dc in next sp, 3 dc in top of ch 3; ch 3, turn. *Row 4:* Work 2 dc in first dc, 3 dc in each sp to corner, work corner in corner sp, 3 dc in each sp to end, 3 dc in top of ch 3. Do not fasten off, but remove hook and set piece and yarn aside. Make 1 triangle each with C, D, and E in same manner.

Assemble frame: Starting with B triangle, insert hook in dropped lp and turn piece to work long edge as follows: Work 2 sc over end of each row (16 sc), draw dropped E lp through lp on hook, sc across long edge of E triangle in same manner; repeat for D, then C triangles; join to first sc on B triangle, forming frame. Fasten off. With matching yarn and working through back lps only, sew frame to edge of small block with B area on block nearest joining of D and E triangles.

Outer Rnds

Now work around entire unit.

Rnd 1: Join A to joining between B and E triangles, ch 4, work 2 tr in same joining; change to F and work 3 dc in each sp along B triangle to corner, work (3 dc, ch 2, 3 dc) in corner sp, work 3 dc in each sp to next joining; with A, work 3 tr in joining; with G, work around C triangle as before; with A, work 3 tr in joining; with H, work around D triangle; with A, work 3 tr in joining; with I, work around E triangle; join to top of ch 4. Fasten off.

Rnd 2: Join A to sp before any 3-tr group, ch 3, work 2 dc in same sp, 3 dc in next sp, * matching colors, work 3 dc in next 3 sp, (3 dc, ch 2, 3 dc) in corner sp, 3 dc in next 3 sp (colored corner made); with A, work 3 dc in next 2 sp; repeat from * around, ending with last colored corner; join. Fasten off.

Rnds 3 through 6: Join A to sp before any A section, ch 3, 2 dc in same sp, 3 dc in next 2 sp, * work colored corner as before; with A, 3 dc in next 3 sp; repeat from * around, ending with colored corner; join. Fasten off. Continue in this manner for 3 more rnds, working colored corners as before and having 1 more 3-dc group in each A section on each rnd.

Rnd 7: With A only, 3 dc in each sp around, working (3 dc, ch 2, 3 dc) in each corner sp. Fasten off.

Joining

To sew: Pin together edges to be sewn. Thread needle with matching yarn. Sew edges with whipstitch working through one or both loops (as desired) of corresponding stitches along adjoining edges. Weave yarn ends through corresponding stitches along adjoining edges.

To crochet: With matching yarn, slip stitch or single crochet through corresponding stitches along adjoining edges.

Sunshine and Shadow

**The dynamic mixture of colors
and textures makes this design
a treat for the eyes.**

Joyce Powell
Honolulu, Hawaii

A few summers ago Joyce came across a checkerboard quilting pattern that intrigued her. The units were the perfect size to translate into granny squares. She used leftover yarn, which accounts for the lovely mixture of colors and textures.

The afghan took almost one year to complete, as Joyce worked on it primarily while riding the bus to and from her job as a receptionist/bookkeeper for a local church community group.

Over the years she has found needlework, including knitting, needlepoint, and cross-stitching, very relaxing. Her mother had tried to teach her to crochet when she was in junior high school but she was "too tense then and the tension of the pieces I was trying to stitch was so tight I couldn't get the hook through the loops." But in college her roommate taught her how to knit. "I enjoyed it so much I decided to give crocheting another chance and have gotten a lot of pleasure out of it since."

SIZE

About 72″ square

MATERIALS

Yarn: Sport weight (see Note below), about 75 oz. assorted colors (A–N) for squares, plus 6 oz. royal blue and 2 oz. purple for border.

Note: Original afghan was worked in medium-weight (sport-weight) scrap yarns of various textures: regular sport yarn, brushed acrylic, and synthetic yarns with silklike sheen. If you, too, use different textures of yarn, be sure to use yarns of same weight and adjust crochet hook size as needed to work all squares to uniform size. See Assembly Diagram (Figure 13) and color key, page 90, for colors used on original, or work colors as desired.

Crochet hook: Size F (4.00 mm) or size that gives you correct gauge.

GAUGE

Each square measures 2″ across.

STITCHES

Ch, sl st, sc, dc, tr

Degree of difficulty: **

Note: Work all rnds from right side.

DIRECTIONS

Basic Square

Make 1,089 squares in all, working 85 A squares, 88 B, 92 C, 96 D, 96 E, 32 F, 88 G, 84 H, 80 I, 36 J, 84 K, 84 L, 84 M, 60 N. Starting at center, ch 6. Join with sl st to form ring.

Rnd 1: Ch 6 (counts as first dc and ch-3 lp), work (3 dc in ring, ch 3) 3 times, 2 dc in ring; join with sl st to 3rd ch of ch 6.

Rnd 2: Ch 3, * work (2 dc, ch 3, 2 dc) over corner lp; working in back lp only of dc, dc in next 3 dc; repeat from * around, ending with dc in last 2 dc; join to top of ch 3. Fasten off.

Assembly

Following Assembly Diagram, crochet squares together, working sc through back lps only from wrong side of work. **Note:** Designer started in center and joined same-colored squares to center, working each added color until she reached outer edge, then finished same-color diagonal strips to corner.

Border

Attach blue to center ch of lp at any corner of afghan.

Rnd 1: Working in back lp only of sts, ch 3, 2 dc in same place, * dc in each ch and dc to next afghan corner lp, work dc in first ch, 3 dc in next ch; repeat from * around, ending with dc in last ch; join to top of ch 3.

Rnd 2: Ch 4, * 3 tr in next dc (corner made), tr in each dc to center dc of 3-dc group at next corner; repeat from * around, ending tr in last dc; join to top of ch 4.

Rnd 3: Ch 3, * dc in each dc around, working 3 dc in center tr at corners; join. Fasten off.

Rnd 4: Attach purple to center dc at any corner, ch 1, 3 sc in same place, sc in each sc around, work 3 sc at each corner; join.

Rnd 5: Sl st to next center corner sc, (ch 4, dc, ch 1, dc) in same sc, work (ch 1, sk 1 sc, dc in next dc) around, working (ch 1, dc) 3 times in center sc at each corner; join to 3rd ch of ch 4. Fasten off.

Rnd 6: Attach blue to last ch-1 sp before any corner, ch 4, * work (dc, ch 1) twice in each of next 2 sp (corner made), work (dc, ch 1) in each sp to next corner; repeat from * around; join to 3rd ch of ch 4.

Rnd 7: Work 2 sc in each sp around; join.

Rnd 8: Sc in each sc around, working 3 sc at corners; join.

Rnd 9 (picot edge): * Sl st in next sc, ch 3, sl st in same sc (picot made), sl st in next sc; repeat from * around. Fasten off.

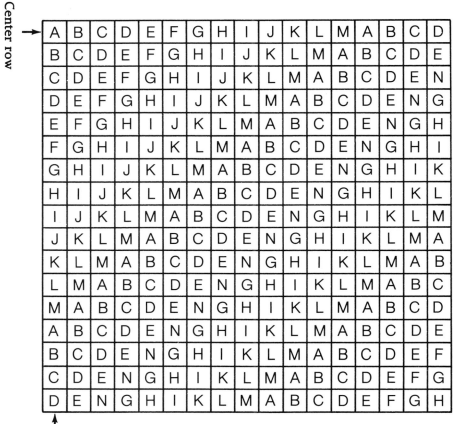

Figure 13. Assembly Diagram

Center row

Center row

Color Key

A Hot pink

B Mauve

C Plum

D Forest green

E Avocado

F Lime green

G Royal blue

H Turquoise

I Navy

J Black

K Violet

L Pale lavender

M Lavender

N Pale mint green

Argyle Granny

For fans of the argyle pattern,
this crocheted version offers a maximum
of design for a minimum of work.

Sarah Elizabeth Farrow
Denver, Colorado

This unique use of the argyle pattern originated with an abandoned Christmas project. Sarah wanted to crochet an unusual argyle sweater for a brother who loves to collect them. She worked out the design, but found that keeping all the different color yarns and bobbins from tangling was just too frustrating. She gave up and made him something else for Christmas. But then when she saw the announcement of the granny-square contest, something clicked. "Why not argyle squares?"

Sarah learned to crochet as a child during the many school vacations she spent with her grandmother. Since Grandma lived in a small town high in the Colorado Rockies, patterns and supplies were difficult to obtain. Sarah therefore learned the virtue of establishing a design with whatever wool happened to be available.

The mother of four boys, including a set of twins, Sarah has put her career as an advertising copywriter on the back burner while she works as a freelance writer at home.

SIZE

Each rectangle measures 3¾" × 6". To make an afghan of the size you desire, see page 165, Designing on Your Own.

MATERIALS

Yarn: Knitting worsted; *for each rectangle:* 15 yd. gray (MC) for background, 9 yd. color A for diamonds, 5 yd. color B for stripes. See page 166 for how to estimate amount of yarn needed for an afghan.

Crochet hook: Size F (4.00 mm) or size that gives you correct gauge.

STITCHES

Ch, sc, dc

Degree of difficulty: ***

DIRECTIONS

Note: Use bobbins if desired. Attach separate yarn for each color area 2 or more sts wide and for stripes. To change colors, work with old color until last 2 lps of last st remain on hook, drop old color to wrong side, with new color yo and draw through lps on hook to complete st, then continue with new color. Drop colors not in use to wrong side of work and pick up when needed on following row.

Rectangle

Starting at lower (narrow edge) with MC, ch 16.

Row 1 (right side): Sc in 2nd ch from hook and in each remaining ch across (15 sc); ch 2, drop MC and attach B; ch 1 (ch 3 just made counts as first dc on following row), turn.

Row 2: Attaching colors as needed, follow first row of chart, Figure 14, working dc in each sc; ch 3, turn. Work in dc and follow chart to top, ending last row with ch 1, turn.

Last row: With MC only, sc in each dc across. Fasten off.

Joining

To sew: Pin together edges to be sewn. Thread needle with matching yarn. Sew edges with whipstitch working through one or both loops (as desired) of corresponding stitches along adjoining edges. Weave yarn ends through corresponding stitches along adjoining edges.

To crochet: With matching yarn, slip stitch or single crochet through corresponding stitches along adjoining edges.

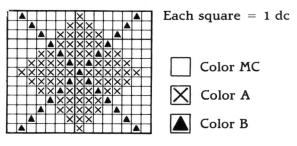

Each square = 1 dc

☐ Color MC

☒ Color A

▲ Color B

Figure 14.

Ohio Stars

**The combination of large and small shapes
executed with an eye for the careful juxtaposition
of color makes this quilt pattern
highly successful in its new translation.**

Barbara B. Weberling
West Melbourne, Florida

Barbara, a Spanish/English teacher with two children, considers crocheting "a form of therapy." Since portability is important to Barbara, she devised a method of starting in the corner of a unit and working on a diagonal that makes switching colors particularly easy. This means that she never has to carry more than a couple of colors with her when she works. A large center block and contrasting small solid- and two-color blocks are joined together for a delightful interplay of shape and color.

Barbara was drawn to the Ohio Star quilt design because she is fascinated by combining elements from different media, especially those having to do with fiber. Her love of texture and yarn has recently resulted in the establishment of a small weaving business. Barbara weaves sweaters, shawls, and ponchos to sell at local boutiques and art shows.

SIZE
About 68″ square

MATERIALS
Yarn: Sport weight, 36 oz. beige (MC), 14 oz. dark rose heather (color A), 16 oz. blue heather (B).

Crochet hook: Size H (5.00 mm) or size that gives you correct gauge.

GAUGE
Large square measures 6″ across; all small squares measure 3″ across.

STITCHES
Ch, sc, reverse sc (directions given below)

Degree of difficulty: ***

DIRECTIONS
Note: All squares are worked in diagonal rows, starting at one corner, increasing to center, then decreasing to form square. For squares to fit together smoothly, work squares to accurate measurements, adjusting number of rows worked if needed.

Large Squares
Make 5 with MC. Starting at one corner with MC, ch 3.

Row 1: Sc in 3rd ch from hook; ch 2, turn.

Row 2: Sk sc, (sc, ch 1, sc) over turning ch at end of row (part of starting ch 3); ch 2, turn.

Row 3: Sc in next ch-1 sp, ch 1, (sc, ch 1, sc) over turning ch; ch 2, turn.

Row 4 (basic inc row): (Sc, ch 1) in each ch-1 sp, (sc, ch 1, sc) over turning ch; ch 2, turn. Repeat Row 4 seventeen times or until side edge measures 6″.

Next row (dec row): (Sc, ch 1) in each ch-1 sp across, ending with sc in last sp; sl st in last sc; ch 2, turn. Repeat last row until 1 sc remains; ch 1, turn. Sl st in last sc. Fasten off.

Small Solid-Color Squares
Make 44 with MC, 32 with color B. Work same as for large square until 11 rows are completed or until side edges measure 3″. Now work dec rows same as for large squares to complete square.

Small Two-Color Squares
Make 136 with MC and A, 184 with MC and B. Starting with MC, work same as small solid-color square until inc rows are completed. Fasten off MC; attach A or B to complete square.

Assembly
Following Assembly Diagram, Figure 15, join squares for center panel (within inner border), sewing square edges neatly together and reversing direction of squares at center to make symmetric design overall.

Inner Border
Rnd 1: Attach MC to any corner of center panel, * (ch 1, sc, ch 1, sc) in corner, (ch 1, sc into edge of work) along panel edge to next corner, spacing sc to keep edge of work flat and smooth (working about 7 sc along side of each small square); repeat from * around; join to first sc.

Rnd 2: (Sc, ch 1) in each ch-1 sp around, working (sc, ch 1) twice in each corner sp; join. Repeat Rnd 2 ten times or until inner border is about 2¼″ wide. Repeat Rnd 2 twice more with A, then once more with

MC (border should be 3″ wide). Fasten off. Following Assembly Diagram, sew remaining squares in place.

Outer Border

Rnd 1: With MC, work (ch 1, sc) around outer edge of afghan, working (ch 1, sc) twice at corners and spacing sc to keep edge flat and smooth; join.

Rnd 2: With A, (ch 1, sc) in each ch-1 sp around, working (ch 1, sc) twice in each corner sp; join.

Rnds 3 through 6: Repeat Rnd 2 once with MC, then 3 times with B. Do not fasten off.

Rnd 7: Ch 1, work sc in sp, ch 1; * insert hook into sp *before* last sc worked, draw up lp, yo and draw through both lps on hook (reverse sc made), ch 1; repeat from * around, working from left to right; join. Fasten off.

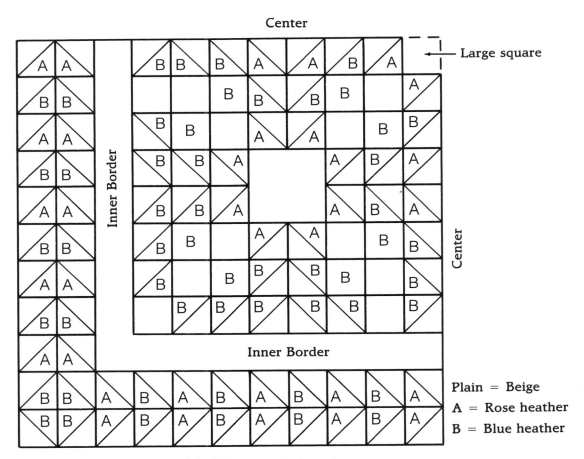

Figure 15. Assembly Diagram (¼ shown)

96

Dimensionals

Dimensionals are patterns containing raised elements that pop out from the background. There are a number of techniques that produce this invigorating textural effect, including looped chain stitches, multiple stitches in a small area, popcorn or other three-dimensional stitches, piggybacking of stitches, or connecting the units in a special manner.

Keely's Strawflower

Inspired by a granddaughter's favorite flower,
the vibrant colors in this design
will set any room ablaze.

Mary Badgerow
Port Huron, Michigan

This spectacular reversible sofa throw was inspired by "the ultimate joy" of Mary Badgerow's life, her granddaughter, Keely. The black graduating to rust, apricot, and orange evokes Keely's favorite flower. By adding a few extra stitches to the traditional granny square, Mary has succeeded in turning it into a hexagon, which suggests the rounded shape of the strawflower. With edges forming a scalloped, petallike border, the effect of color and shape is nothing less than sensational.

Mary first began to crochet when her son and daughter were small, learning from magazines, particularly old issues of *Woman's Day*. In the '70s she enjoyed macramé, then moved on to oil paintings of sunsets, landscapes, and houses.

A retired hostess/cashier at a local restaurant, former real estate broker, and hospice volunteer, Mary still loves to get up at 4:30 in the morning to crochet, claiming that "time is of the essence." Without any distractions, she completed this throw in just three weeks.

SIZE

About 52″ × 62″

MATERIALS

Yarn: Knitting worsted, 21½ oz. black (color A), 15 oz. red brown (B), 7 oz. each white (C), apricot (D), and rust (E)

Crochet hooks: Sizes G and I (4.50 and 5.50 mm) or sizes that give you correct gauge.

GAUGE

With smaller hook, each hexagon measures 6½″ across from side to side.

STITCHES

Ch, sl st, sc, dc, pc, and long dc (directions given below)

Degree of difficulty: ***

DIRECTIONS

Note: Work all rnds from right side.

Plain Hexagons

Make 54. Starting at center with color B and smaller hook, ch 6. Join with sl st to form ring.

Rnd 1: Work 2 sc in each ch around (12 sc); do not join yet. Fasten off B; attach C and with C, join to first sc.

Rnd 2: Ch 3, dc in same sc, work 2 dc in each remaining sc (24 dc, counting ch 3 as first dc). Fasten off C; attach B and join to top of ch 3.

Rnd 3: Ch 1, sc in each dc around. Fasten off B; attach D and join to first sc.

Rnd 4: Repeat Rnd 2 (48 dc). Fasten off D; attach E and join to top of ch 3.

Rnd 5: Ch 3, dc in next dc and in each remaining dc around. Fasten off E; attach B and join to top of ch 3.

Rnd 6: With B, ch 3, dc in same place, * dc in next 7 dc, 2 dc in next dc; repeat from * around, ending with dc in last 7 dc. Fasten off B; attach A and join.

Rnd 7: Ch 3, 3 dc in sp between ch 3 and dc (first corner made), * dc in next 9 dc, 3 dc in next sp between 2 dc; repeat from * around, ending with dc in last 8 dc (6 corners made); join. Fasten off.

Popcorn Hexagon

Make 22.

Rnds 1 through 3: With smaller hook, work same as for plain hexagon through Rnd 3, but working Rnd 1 with B, Rnd 2 with D, Rnd 3 with B. Fasten off B; attach C and join.

Rnd 4: Ch 3, 4 dc in same place as joining, drop lp from hook, insert hook front to back through top of ch 3 and pull dropped lp through (first popcorn, pc, made), * ch 4, sk 1 sc, 5 dc in next sc, drop lp from hook, insert hook in first dc of 5-dc group and draw dropped lp through (another pc made); repeat from * around, ending with ch 4. Fasten off C; attach B and join to top of first pc.

Rnd 5: Ch 3, dc over first ch-4 lp, yo and draw up long lp in Rnd 3 sc (between pc), (yo and draw through 2 lps on hook) twice (long dc made enclosing ch-4 lp in st), work 2 more regular dc over same lp, * work (2 dc, long dc as before, 2 dc) over next lp; repeat from * around; join.

Rnd 6: Ch 3, dc in each st around. Fasten off B; attach A and join.

Rnd 7: Ch 3, * 3 dc in next dc (corner made), dc in next 9 dc; repeat from * around, ending with dc in last 8 dc; join. Fasten off.

Assembly

See Assembly Diagram, Figure 16, for placement of hexagons (1 on diagram indicates plain hexagon, 2 indicates popcorn hexagon). Hold pieces with right sides together and sew adjoining edges together through back lps only of corresponding sts.

Border

Attach A to any outer corner along afghan edge.

Rnd 1: Working with larger hook, ch 3, dc in each dc around, decreasing at inner corners (at joinings) as follows: Work to last st before joining, work (yo and draw up lp in next st, yo and draw through first 2 lps on hook) twice, yo and draw through all lps on hook. Join to top of ch 3.

Rnd 2: Ch 3, dc around as before, decreasing at inner corners and, if needed to keep border flat, increasing at outer corners, working 2 dc in 1 dc; join. Fasten off.

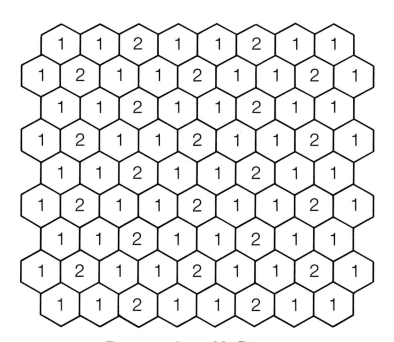

Figure 16. Assembly Diagram

1 = **Plain hexagon**

2 = **Popcorn hexagon**

Star Flowers

Made of looped chain stitches,
these colorful, three-dimensional
flowers look fresh enough to pick.

Jean Beauchamp
Humble, Texas

These gently colored octagons in lilac, mint green, pink, and yellow are worked from the outside of the unit in toward the center. The bold raised effect is a result of chains that are looped through one another and brought together in the center to form a flower. The scalloped lavender border follows the shape of the units and gives a flowing, graceful line to the whole.

Jean, a busy sales representative with five children and eight grandchildren, crocheted this afghan for her mother, who lives in a nursing home. Hoping to help her feel more comfortable and make her room more homey, she selected colors to complement the room. The design is one she had been using for years on Christmas potholders. Crocheting a little each evening after work, she finished just in time to enter the contest.

SIZE
About 44″ × 76″

MATERIALS
Yarn: Knitting worsted, 18 oz. lilac (MC) for fill-in motifs and afghan border, 9 oz. lavender (color A); 6 oz. each baby pink (B) and medium pink (C); 4 oz. each white (D), mint green (E), baby blue (F), yellow (G) for octagons.

Crochet hook: Size K (6.50 mm) or size that gives you correct gauge.

GAUGE
Each octagon measures 8″ across from side to side; fill-in motifs measure 4″ across.

STITCHES
Ch, sl st, sc, dc

Degree of difficulty: ***

DIRECTIONS
Note: Work all rnds from right side. Reserve 4 oz. of color A to use for octagon borders. Begin each octagon with B or C, then use a different color (A, D, E, F, or G) for each of the remaining rounds. Distribute colors evenly throughout afghan.

Octagons
Make 45, varying color combinations and sequence for each. Starting at *outer* edge of octagon, using B or C, loosely ch 64 to measure about 22″ long. Join with sl st to form large ring (do not twist sts). **Note:** Octagon will be a loose circle until loops are drawn one through another after last rnd is completed.

Rnd 1: Ch 3, dc in next 7 ch of ring, ch 10, (dc in next 8 ch of ring, ch 10) 7 times (8 ch-10 lps made); join with sl st to top of starting ch 3. Fasten off. Attach any different octagon color to first dc after joining.

Rnd 2: Ch 3, dc in next 5 dc, * ch 10, sk 1 dc before and after lp of previous rnd, dc in next 6 dc; repeat from * around, ending with ch 10; join to top of starting ch 3. Fasten off; attach next color to first dc after joining.

Rnd 3: Ch 3, dc in next 3 dc, * ch 10, sk 1 dc before and after lp of previous rnd, dc in next 4 dc; repeat from * around, ending with ch 10; join. Fasten off; attach next color to first dc after joining.

Rnd 4: Ch 3, dc in next dc, * ch 10, sk 1 dc before and after lp of previous rnd, dc in next 2 dc; repeat from * around, ending with ch 10; join. Fasten off.

Loops: Starting from outer edge, draw Rnd-2 lp through corresponding Rnd-1 lp, then working toward center, draw Rnd-3 lp through Rnd 2-lp, the Rnd-4 lp through Rnd-3 lp. Work around octagon, drawing each set of lps through toward center. Cut 6″ length of color yarn used on Rnd 4. With crochet hook or yarn needle draw yarn through all Rnd-4 lps in order; tie tightly and securely together at center. Weave in yarn ends to conceal them.

Octagon border: With A, crochet a rnd of sc around octagon, working into unworked side of foundation chain.

Fill-in Motifs
Make 32. Starting at outer edge with MC, loosely ch 32 to measure about 10″ long. Join with sl st to form ring.

Rnd 1: Ch 3, dc in next 3 ch of ring, ch 8,

(dc in next 4 ch, ch 8) 7 times (8 ch-8 lps made); join with sl st to top of starting ch 3. Fasten off. With matching yarn, draw lps together at center as for octagon.

Border: With MC, crochet a rnd of sc around motif, working in unworked side of foundation chain.

Assembly
Balancing colors throughout, arrange octagons in 5 rows of 9 each. Sew adjoining sides together through back lps only of corresponding sts. In same manner, sew fill-in motifs to open areas where 4 octagons meet.

Afghan Border
Attach MC to any st along edge. Working in back loop only, work 4 rnds of sc around afghan, increasing as needed (*to inc,* work 2 sc in 1 sc) to keep outward curved edges flat and decreasing (*to dec,* skip 1 sc) at indentations where octagons are joined.

Wedding White

Made especially for the occasion,
this white-on-white wedding bedcover
has love crocheted in every stitch.

Janet M. Crawford
Waltham, Massachusetts

Our third-prize winner is a double bed throw made for the artist's sister. Done all in white, adorned with popcorn stitches, lacy mesh, and scalloped edges, it is a stunning example of the excitement texture can create. Janet had looked through many magazines trying to find a pattern she liked. In the end, she took a little from here and a little from there and came up with this romantically beautiful combination of elements that is entirely her own.

Janet's mother taught her how to crochet when she was about six years old. "I was sick a lot as a child and crocheting would keep me busy for hours." Today Janet keeps busy working as an interior designer, painting in watercolors and acrylics, and acting with a community theater group. With a built-in deadline for finishing the gift—her sister's wedding day—Janet felt pressed for time. So she began to crochet the squares during her lunch hour and at rehearsals of her play. She made her deadline, and her sister's pleasure made it all worthwhile.

SIZE

About 94″ × 108″

MATERIALS

Yarn: Knitting worsted, 189 oz. (54 3½-oz. skeins) white

Crochet hook: Size H (5.00 mm) or size that gives you correct gauge.

GAUGE

Each square measures about 14″ across.

STITCHES

Ch, sl st, sc, dc, hdc, pc (directions given below)

Degree of difficulty: ****

DIRECTIONS

Note: Dense popcorn sections may bulge slightly when squares are joined.

Work all rnds from right side.

Squares

Make 42. Starting at center, ch 6. Join with sl st to form ring.

Rnd 1: Ch 1, work 12 sc in ring; join to first sc.

Rnd 2: Ch 1, sc in each sc around (12 sc); from now on do not join, but work around and around. Mark beg of rnds.

Rnd 3: * (Dc, ch 1, dc) in next sc, dc in next 2 sc; repeat from * around.

Rnd 4: * (2 dc, ch 1, 2 dc) in next ch-1 sp, dc in next sp between 2 dc, 5 dc in next sp, drop lp from hook, insert hook in first dc of 5-dc group and draw dropped lp through (popcorn, pc, made), dc in next sp; repeat from * around (4 pc made).

Rnd 5: * Sk 1 dc, dc in next dc, (2 dc, ch 1, 2 dc) in next ch-1 sp (corner made), sk 1 dc, dc in next dc, dc in next sp, pc in next 2

sp (pc made before and after pc of previous rnd), dc in next sp; repeat from * around.

Rnd 6: * Sk 1 dc, dc in next 2 dc, (2 dc, ch 1, 2 dc) in next ch-1 sp (corner made in corner sp), sk 1 dc, dc in next 2 dc, dc in next sp, pc in next 3 sp, dc in next sp; repeat from * around.

Rnd 7: * Sk 1 dc, dc in each dc to corner sp, work corner in corner sp, sk 1 dc, dc in each dc to within 1 dc of next pc, dc in sp before next dc, pc in sp before pc, pc in each sp between pc, pc in next sp (there is 1 pc more than on previous rnd), dc in next sp; repeat from * around.

Rnds 8 and 9: Repeat Rnd 7 (6 pc in each section on Rnd 9).

Rnd 10: * Work around corner as before to within 1 dc of next pc, dc in next sp, ch 2, sk 1 sp, pc in each sp between 2 pc (5 pc made), ch 2, sk 1 sp, dc in next sp (mesh made); repeat from * around, ending with last pc, ch 2, sk 2 sp, dc in next sp (1 mesh made before and after each pc section).

Rnd 11: * Work around corner as before to within 2 dc before next mesh, dc in next sp, ch 2, dc in next mesh, ch 2, pc in each sp between 2 pc (4 pc made), ch 2, dc in mesh, ch 2, sk 1 sp, dc in next sp (2 meshes each side of pc section); repeat from * around, ending with dc in last mesh.

Rnd 12: Ch 2, sk 1 sp, dc in next sp (1 more mesh made), * work around corner to within 2 dc before next mesh, dc in next sp, (ch 2, dc) in each mesh, ch 2, pc in each sp between 2 pc (1 pc less than on previous rnd), (ch 2, dc) in each remaining mesh, ch 2, sk 1 sp, dc in next sp (1 mesh more each side of pc sections); repeat from * around, ending dc in last mesh before marker.

Rnd 13: Work 2 more meshes, then work as from * of Rnd 12 around.

Rnd 14: Work 3 more meshes, then work as from * of Rnd 12.

Rnd 15: Work 4 more meshes, * work corner as before, work 11 meshes; repeat from * 4 times, continuing on past marker to work meshes, then dc to within 2 dc of first corner sp, hdc in next dc, sc in next dc.

Rnd 16: Sc in each dc and ch all around edge, working 5 sc in each corner sp; join to first sc. Fasten off.

Assembly

To join, hold 2 squares right sides together and, inserting hook under both lps of corresponding sts, sc squares together along one edge. Join squares in this manner to form 6 strips of 7 squares each; then join strips.

Border

Join yarn to center sc at any corner of afghan.

Rnd 1: Ch 4, dc in same sc (first corner made), * work (ch 1, sk 1 sc, dc in next sc) across edge of afghan to next corner sc (see Note below), ch 1, work (dc, ch 1, dc) in corner sc; repeat from * around, ending with ch 1; join to 3rd ch of ch 4.

Note: Adjust spacing of sts so there is a ch-1 sp at each corner, 162 sp along each 6-square edge and 192 sp (27 or 28 sp each square) along each 7-square edge between corners.

Rnd 2: Sl st in corner sp, ch 3, 4 dc, drop lp from hook, insert hook in top of ch 3, draw dropped lp through (first pc made), ch

4, * work (5-dc pc as for squares in next ch-1 sp, ch 3, sk 1 sp) to next corner, pc in corner sp, ch 4, do not sk next sp; repeat from * around, ending ch 3, sk last sp; join to top of first pc.

Rnd 3: Sc in same pc, * sc in first ch of ch 4, pc in next ch, sc in next 2 ch, sc in next pc, (sc in next 3 ch, sc in next pc) twice, **sc in next ch, pc in next ch, sc in next ch, (sc in next pc, sc in next 3 ch) 4 times, sc in next pc***; repeat from ** to *** to next corner ch-4 lp; repeat from * around, ending with sc in last ch; join to first sc.

Rnd 4: Sc in first 2 sc, ch 1, sk pc, 3 sc in next sc, * sc in next sc, 2 sc in next sc, sc in next sc, ** ch 1, sk 1 sc, sc in next 7 sc, ch 1, sk pc, sc in next 7 sc, ch 1, sk 1 sc, sc in next 3 sc; repeat from ** to last 7 sts before corner pc, sc in next 7 sc, ch 1 (corner ch 1 made), sk pc, 3 sc in next sc ***; repeat from * to *** around, ending with sc in last 5 sts.

Rnd 5: Sk first sc, sc in next sc, * sc in ch, sc in next sc, pc in next sc, sc in next 2 sc, ** 2 sc in next sc, sc in next sc, 2 sc in next sc, ch 2, sk ch and 1 sc, sc in next 4 sc, pc in next sc, sc in next sc, sc in ch, sc in next sc, pc in next sc, sc in next 4 sc, ch 2, sk sc and ch; repeat from ** to last 5 sc before next corner ch 1, 2 sc in sc, sc in 2 sc, pc in next sc, sc in next sc ***; repeat from * to *** around, ending with pc in skipped first st; join.

Rnd 6: Sc in first 3 sc, * ch 1, sk pc, sc in next 2 sc, ** 2 dc in next sc, dc in next 3 sc, 2 dc in next sc, ch 3, sk ch and 1 sc, (sc in 3 sc, ch 1, sk pc) twice, sc in next 3 sc, ch 3, sk sc and ch; repeat from ** to last 3 sc before next corner pc, 2 dc in next sc, sc in

next 2 sc, ch 1, sk pc, sc in next 3 sc ***; repeat from * to *** around, ending with ch 1, sk last pc; join.

Rnd 7: Sc in first sc, pc in next sc, sc in next sc, sc in ch, sc in next 2 sc, * 2 dc in next dc, dc in next 5 dc, 2 dc in next dc, ch 3, sk ch and 1 sc, sc in 2 sc, sc in ch, sc in next sc, pc in next sc, sc in next sc, sc in ch, sc in next 2 sc, ch 3; repeat from * to last dc before corner, 2 dc in last dc, sc in next 2 sc, sc in ch, sc in next sc, pc in next sc, sc in next sc, sc in ch, sc in next 2 sc **; repeat from * to ** around, ending with sc in last ch; join.

Rnd 8: Sc in first sc, ch 1, sk pc, sc in 3 sc, 2 sc in next sc, * work 2 dc in next dc, dc in 7 dc, 2 dc in next dc, ch 3, sk ch and sc, sc in 3 sc, ch 1, sk pc, sc in 3 sc, ch 3; repeat from * to last dc before next corner, work 2 dc in this last dc, then 2 sc in next sc, sc in 3 sc, ch 1, sk pc, sc in 3 sc, 2 sc in next sc **; repeat from * to ** around, ending with sc in last 2 sc; join.

Rnd 9: Sc in first 6 sts, 2 sc in next sc, * 2 dc in next dc, dc in 9 dc, 2 dc in next dc, ch 3, sk ch and 1 sc, sc in 5 sts, ch 3; repeat from * to last dc before next corner, work 2 dc in last dc, 2 sc in next sc, sc in 9 sts, 2 sc in next sc **; repeat from * to ** around, ending sc in last 3 sc; join.

Rnd 10: Sc in first sc, (ch 3, sk 1 sc, sc in next sc) twice, ch 3, sk 3 sc, * sc in next dc, (ch 3, sk 2 dc, sc in next dc) 4 times, ch 3, sk ch and 1 sc, sc in 3 sc, ch 3; repeat from * to last dc before next corner, sc in dc, (ch 3, sk 1 sc, sc in next sc) 5 times, ch 3, sk 3 sc **; repeat from * to ** around, ending ch 3; join to first sc.

Rnd 11: Sl st to center of next ch-3 sp, ch 3 and work 4 dc to make first pc, (ch 3, pc in next sp) 6 times, * ch 5, sc in center sc of 3-sc group, ch 5, sk sc and ch 3, pc in next ch-3 sp, (ch 3, pc in next sp) 3 times; repeat from * around, working (ch 3, pc) in each sp around corners; join to top of pc.

Rnd 12: Sc in first pc, * sc in next ch, (sc, ch 1, sc) in next ch, sc in next ch, sc in next pc; repeat from * to next ch 5, sc in next 5 ch, sc in sc, sc in next 5 ch, sc in pc **; repeat from * to ** around, ending with sc in last ch; join to first sc. Fasten off.

Rose-Shaded Fantasy

The stunning arrangement of mauve
and ivory gives these squares
a contemporary appeal.

Gail Tanquary
San Leandro, California

Gail might never have been a crocheter had she not been a tomboy at age nine. That was before the women's movement, and her neighbor, a "Mrs. B," thought Gail and her girlfriends most unladylike to want to wear jeans and climb trees. So she gathered them up and taught them to crochet.

Although they thought Mrs. B much too stern, this is a fond memory for Gail, who eventually turned her needlecraft skills into a successful business.

In 1973, when her husband started an art gallery and custom picture-framing operation, she joined him, taking part of the space for a yarn shop. The enterprise has been successful enough for them to raise three daughters, two of whom are now in college. "We both teach classes and offer instructions. Running the shop has been a good way to put an interest in knitting and crochet to work for us."

SIZE

Each square measures about 9½" across. To make an afghan of the size you desire, see page 165, Designing on Your Own.

MATERIALS

Yarn: Sport weight; *for each square:* 40 yd. dark rose (color A), 32 yd. medium rose (B), 18 yd. pale rose (C). See page 166 for how to estimate amount of yarn needed for an afghan.

Crochet hook: Size I (5.50 mm) or size that gives correct gauge.

STITCHES

Ch, sl st, sc, dc, d tr

Degree of difficulty: ***

DIRECTIONS

Note: Work all rnds from right side.

Square

Starting at center with color A, ch 6. Join with sl st to form ring.

Rnd 1: Ch 3 (counts as first dc), work 2 dc in ring, (ch 3, 3 dc in ring) 3 times, ch 3; join to top of first ch 3.

Rnd 2: Sl st to next corner ch-3 lp, ch 3, work (2 dc, ch 3, 3 dc) over same corner lp (first corner made), * ch 1, (3 dc, ch 3, 3 dc) over next corner lp; repeat from * around, ending with ch 1; join to top of ch 3.

Rnd 3: Sl st to next corner lp, work first corner, * 3 dc in next ch-1 sp, work corner over next corner lp; repeat from * around, ending with 3 dc in last ch-1 sp; join to top of ch 3.

Rnd 4: Ch 1, sc in same place as joining, sc in each dc around and work (2 sc, ch 1, 2 sc) over each corner lp; join to first sc.

Rnd 5: Ch 1, sc in each sc around and work (sc, ch 1, sc) over each corner ch-1 lp; join to first sc.

Rnds 6 and 7: Repeat Rnd 5 (19 sc each side after Rnd 7 is completed). Fasten off A; attach B to any corner lp.

Rnd 8: With B, ch 1, * work (sc, ch 1, sc) in corner lp, sc in next 9 sc, work d tr (see page 163) around post (see page 164) of dc 4 rows below next sc (dc is center dc of 3-dc group on Rnd 3), sk the sc behind d tr, sc in next 9 sc; repeat from * around; join to first sc.

Rnd 9: Sl st to corner ch-1 lp, * work corner, sc in next 9 sc, d tr around post of sc 4 rows below next sc, sc in top of d tr of previous rnd, d tr around post of sc 4 rows below next sc, skip sc behind d tr just made, sc in next 9 sc (d tr made on each side of previous d tr); repeat from * around; join. Fasten off B; attach C to any corner ch-1 lp.

Rnd 10: With C, * work corner, sc in 9 sc, d tr around post of sc 4 rows below next sc, sk sc behind d tr just made, sc in each d tr and sc to next d tr, work sc in d tr, work d tr around post of sc 4 rows below next sc, sk sc behind d tr, sc in last 9 sc to corner lp; repeat from * around; join.

Rnd 11: Sl st to corner lp and work as for Rnd 10. Fasten off C; attach B to any corner lp.

Rnds 12 and 13: With B, repeat Rnds 10 and 11. Fasten off B; attach A to any corner lp.

Rnd 14: With A, repeat Rnd 10. Fasten off.

Joining

To sew: Pin together edges to be sewn. Thread needle with matching yarn. Sew edges with whipstitch working through one or both loops (as desired) of corresponding stitches along adjoining edges.

To crochet: With matching yarn, slip stitch or single crochet through corresponding stitches along adjoining edges.

Pink Popcorn Hearts

These lovely hearts make a
three-dimensional valentine
that excites the eye.

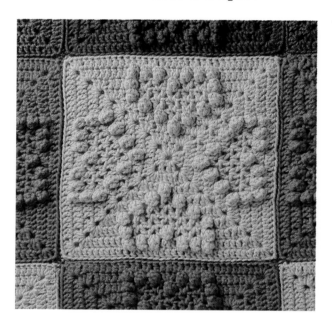

Janet Casey
Ft. Myers, Florida

Janet Casey collects hearts and when her son Joshua suggested she make an afghan with this motif, she thought it was a fine idea, since she already had the yarn. Her aunt had given it to her as a gift to make something for herself. The subtle colors, harmoniously graduating from tea rose to burgundy, were perfect for the design.

Janet enjoys needlepoint, macramé, and cross-stitch but crocheting is her favorite hobby, which she pursues when her workday at the local pharmacy has ended. She was taught the basic chain, single crochet, and double crochet stitches by her grandmother when she was eight years old, "but then my grandma had to go and check the potatoes so I taught myself the rest. Now Grandma comes to me to ask how to do a stitch."

SIZE

Each square measures 10″ across. To make an afghan of the size you desire, see page 165, Designing on Your Own.

MATERIALS

Yarn: Knitting worsted; *for each square:* 110 yd. (1¾ oz.—a 3½-oz. skein will make 2 squares). See page 166 for how to estimate amount of yarn needed for an afghan.

Crochet hook: Size H (5.00 mm) or size that gives you correct gauge.

STITCHES

Ch, sl st, dc, pc, and V-st (directions given below)

Degree of difficulty: ****

DIRECTIONS

Note: Work all rnds from right side.

Square

Starting at center, ch 6. Join with sl st to form ring.

Rnd 1: Ch 3 (counts as first dc), 2 dc in ring, ch 2, (3 dc in ring, ch 2) 3 times; join with sl st to top of ch 3.

Rnd 2: Sl st to next ch-2 lp, ch 3, (2 dc, ch 2, 3 dc) over same lp (first corner made), * dc in next 3 dc, (3 dc, ch 2, 3 dc) over next lp (another corner made); repeat from * around, ending with dc in last 3 dc; join.

Rnd 3: Sl st to first corner lp, work first corner as before, * sk 1 dc, dc in next 2 dc, ch 1, sk 1 dc; work popcorn (pc) as follows: Work 4 dc in next st, drop lp from hook, insert hook through top of first dc and draw dropped lp through (pc made); ch 1, sk 1 dc, dc in next 2 dc, sk 1 dc, work another corner as before over corner lp; repeat from

* around, ending with dc in 2 dc, sk last dc; join.

Rnd 4: Sl st to first corner lp, * work corner over corner lp, sk 1 dc, dc in next dc, ch 1, sk 1 dc, pc in next dc, ch 1, sk 1 dc and ch, (dc, ch 1, dc) in top of pc (V-st made), ch 1, sk ch and 1 dc, pc in next dc, ch 1, sk 1 dc, dc in next dc, sk 1 dc; repeat from * around; join.

Rnd 5: Sl st to first corner lp, * work corner, dc in next dc, ch 1, sk 1 dc, pc in next dc, ch 1, V-st in next pc, V-st in next ch-1 sp of V-st, V-st in next pc, ch 1, sk ch and 1 dc, pc in next dc, ch 1, sk 1 dc, dc in next dc; repeat from * around; join.

Rnd 6: Sl st to corner lp, * work corner, dc in first dc, ch 1, sk 1 dc, pc in next dc, ch 1, V-st in next pc, V-st in next 3 V-sts, V-st in next pc, ch 1, sk ch and 1 dc, pc in next dc, ch 1, sk 1 dc, dc in dc; repeat from * around; join.

Rnd 7: Sl st to first corner lp, * work corner, sk next dc, dc in next 3 dc, ch 1, pc in next pc, ch 1, V-st in next 2 V-sts, ch 1, pc in next V-st, ch 1, V-st in next 2 V-sts, ch 1, pc in next pc, ch 1, dc in next 3 dc, sk next dc; repeat from * around; join.

Rnd 8: Sl st to first corner lp, * work corner, sk 1 dc, dc in next 5 dc, ch 1, pc in next pc, (ch 1, pc) in next 2 V-sts, ch 1, 3 dc in next pc, (ch 1, pc) in next 2 V-sts, ch 1, pc in next pc, ch 1, dc in next 5 dc, sk 1 dc; repeat from * around; join.

Rnd 9: Sl st to first corner lp, * work corner, sk 1 dc, dc in 7 dc, dc in next sp (before pc), 2 dc in next 2 sp, dc in next sp, dc in next 3 dc, dc in next sp, 2 dc in next 2 sp, dc in next sp (after pc), dc in next 7 dc, sk 1 dc; repeat from * around; join. Fasten off.

Joining

To sew: Pin together edges to be sewn. Thread needle with matching yarn. Sew edges with whipstitch working through one or both loops (as desired) of corresponding stitches along adjoining edges. Weave yarn ends through corresponding stitches along adjoining edges.

To crochet: With matching yarn, slip stitch or single crochet through corresponding stitches along adjoining edges.

Triple Delight

A traditional square adorned with an
untraditional chain and loop makes
this attractive pattern much easier
to execute than you would expect.

Judy Lewis
Mountain Home, Arkansas

Judy has been crocheting for thirty years, and she is just "tickled"
over the recognition she has won in *Woman's Day*'s contest. She has
become something of a town celebrity since her afghan was featured in
the magazine and someone brought it to the attention of the local radio
station. Hats off to this mother of five and grandmother of five whose
richly textured pattern in bright pink, slate blue, beige, and cream captured the judges' eyes.

The square is begun in the center, like a traditional square, but then
long chains are added at the corners and looped in the center for a
three-dimensional effect.

SIZE

Each square measures 5½" across. To make an afghan of the size you desire, see page 165, Designing on Your Own.

MATERIALS

Yarn: Knitting worsted; *for each square:* 3 yd. bright pink (color A), 7 yd. each cream (B) and beige (C), 19 yd. slate blue (D). See page 166 for how to estimate amount of yarn needed for an afghan.

Crochet hook: Size G (4.50 mm) or size that gives you correct gauge.

STITCHES

Ch, sl st, dc

Degree of difficulty: ***

DIRECTIONS

Note: Square will appear quite loose until loops at corners are drawn one through another after Rnd 5 is completed.

Work all rnds from right side.

Square

Starting at center with color A, ch 4. Join with sl st to form ring.

Rnd 1: Ch 3 (counts as first dc), 2 dc in ring, ch 8, (3 dc in ring, ch 8) 3 times; join to top of ch 3 (4 ch-8 lps made). Fasten off.

Rnd 2: With B, join yarn with sl st in back of center dc of 3-dc group (near base of st), ch 12, (sl st in back of center dc of next 3-dc group, ch 12) 3 times; join to first sl st.

Rnd 3: Ch 3, holding Rnd-1 sts forward out of way, work 2 dc over first ch-12 lp, ch 12, work 3 dc over end of same lp, ch 1, * work (3 dc, ch 12, 3 dc, ch 1) over next ch-12 lp; repeat from * twice more; join to top of ch 3. Fasten off.

Rnd 4: With C, sl st in any ch-1 sp, ch 3, work 2 dc in same sp, ch 1, * work (3 dc, ch 12, 3 dc, ch 1) over next ch-12 lp (corner made), work (3 dc, ch 1) in next ch-1 sp; repeat from * around, work corner; join to top of ch 3. Fasten off.

Rnd 5: With D, sl st in last ch-1 sp before any corner, ch 3, 2 dc in same sp, * work (3 dc, ch 12, 3 dc) over corner lp, 3 dc in each ch-1 sp to next corner; repeat from * twice more, work corner, 3 dc in last ch-1 sp; join. Do not fasten off. At each corner, start at center bringing Rnd-2 lp up through Rnd-1 lp, then work out to edge, bringing Rnd-3 lp through Rnd-2 lp, Rnd-4 lp through Rnd-3 lp, Rnd-5 lp through Rnd-4 lp, forming chain from center to each corner. On each rnd, slide dc groups toward base of lp.

Rnd 6: Still with D, ch 3, * dc in each dc to corner lp, work 1 dc over D corner lp *before* C lp, work (3 dc, ch 3, 3 dc) on center part of D lp brought through previous C lp, work 1 dc over same corner lp *after* C lp; repeat from * 3 times, dc in last 6 dc; join. Fasten off.

Joining

To sew: Pin together edges to be sewn. Thread needle with matching yarn. Sew edges with whipstitch working through one or both loops (as desired) of corresponding stitches along adjoining edges. Weave yarn ends through corresponding stitches along adjoining edges.

To crochet: With matching yarn, slip stitch or single crochet through corresponding stitches along adjoining edges.

Raised Chevron

**A dramatic progression of color and
an imaginative combination of stitches
result in an exquisite design.**

Delma A. Myers
Anchorage, Alaska

Now that Delma's four children are grown, she works full time as a drafter in the engineering department of the Anchorage Telephone Utility. She and her husband, Doug, are active in a local Mustang club and participate in car shows and parades. She is also a member of the Anchorage Community Chorus, and has performed with them at Lincoln Center and Carnegie Hall in New York City, and also in Eastern Europe, England, Scotland, and Canada.

Even so, she still finds time to enjoy needlework, including needlepoint, bargello, crewel embroidery, latch hook, and sewing. Her favorite is crochet, which she has done for about thirty years, winning ribbons at state fairs and festivals in the process. The inspiration for this dramatic pillow came from an old-fashioned pattern book. Since turquoise is Delma's favorite color, she chose several shades of it, creating an exciting three-dimensional effect by her splendid arrangement of color—from the dark center of the square to its light rim.

SIZE

The pillow measures 15″ × 15″. If you wish to make an afghan, see page 165, Designing on Your Own.

MATERIALS

Yarn: Knitting worsted; *for each square:* 48 yd. teal (color A), 80 yd. pale aqua (B), 47 yd. aqua (C), 72 yd. turquoise (D). See page 166 for how to estimate amount of yarn needed for an afghan.

Crochet hook: Size H (5.00 mm) or size that gives you correct gauge.

STITCHES

Ch, sl st, sc, hdc, dc, tr tr

Degree of difficulty: ***

DIRECTIONS

Note: Work all rnds from right side.

Square

Starting at center with A, ch 4. Join with sl st to form ring.

Rnd 1: Ch 1, 8 sc in ring; join with sl st to first sc.

Rnd 2: Ch 1, sc in first 2 sc, * (sc, ch 3, sc) in next sc (corner made), sc in next sc; repeat from * twice, (sc, ch 3) in same place as first sc; join to first sc.

Rnds 3 through 13: Ch 1, reaching backwards, sc over corner lp just completed, * sc in each sc to next corner lp, (sc, ch 3, sc) over corner lp; repeat from * around, ending sc to last sc, (sc, ch 3) over first corner lp; join. Repeat Rnd 3 ten times more. Fasten off. Attach B to any corner lp.

Rnd 14: Ch 1, sc over same corner lp, * sc in next 12 sc, work tr tr (see page 163) around post (see page 164) of sc 4 rows below next sc, sk sc behind tr tr, sc in next 12

sc, (sc, ch 3, sc) over corner lp; repeat from * around, ending with (sc, ch 3) in first corner; join.

Rnd 15: Ch 1, reaching backwards, sc over corner lp just completed, * sc in next 12 sc, work tr tr around post of sc 4 rows below next sc, always skip sc behind tr tr just worked throughout, sc in next st, work tr tr as before below next sc, sc in next 12 sc, work corner as before; repeat from * around, ending with (sc, ch 3) in first corner; join.

Rnd 16: * Work corner as before, sc in next 12 sc, tr tr below next sc, sc in each st to next tr tr, sc in tr tr, tr tr below next sc, sc in next 12 sc; repeat from * around, ending with (sc, ch 3) in first corner; join. Fasten off B. Attach C to any corner.

Rnds 17 through 20: With C, work as for Rnd 16 for 4 rnds. Fasten off C. Attach D to any corner.

Rnds 21 through 25: With D, work as for Rnd 16 for 5 rnds. Fasten off. Attach B to any corner.

Rnd 26: With B, ch 1, sc in last ch of corner lp just completed, * working in back lp only, sc in each sc and tr tr to next corner lp, sc in next ch, ch 2, sc in next ch; repeat from * around, ending sc in next ch of first corner lp, ch 2; join.

Rnd 27: Ch 1, reaching backwards, sl st in nearest ch of corner lp, ch 2 (counts as first hdc), * working in back lp only, hdc in each st around, working (hdc in first ch, ch 2, hdc in 2nd ch) at each corner, ending with (hdc, ch 2) at first corner; join.

Rnd 28: Repeat last rnd once more. Fasten off.

Florals

The patterns in this section have fabulous flower designs as their major element. Many of these glorious displays of color were inspired by nature. Flowers appear large and small, bold and dainty, and show a remarkable variety of stitches.

Bold Octagons with Tiny Diamonds

A combination of large and small units
with bold, blazing color makes this
radiant design a third-prize winner!

Leslie Sternberger
Knoxville, Tennessee

Leslie Sternberger made this prizewinning afghan as a sophomore at
Hiwassee Junior College. She explains that the school, "in a rural setting
here in Tennessee, did not provide much in the way of social entertain-
ment for its students. So instead of watching TV or reading, I used my
crochet hooks, especially during the winter months." Leslie is used to
entertaining herself this way, having grown up in a rural community in
Arkansas. She learned to crochet from a neighbor whose favorite pattern
was the "snowflake" because no two were ever alike. This concept appealed to Leslie because she gets bored with repetitive designs.

A practical person, Leslie always saved the remnants of yarn from
other projects, and now has so much she keeps them in thirty-gallon
trash cans. So she just dipped into her reservoir of colors and decided to
use the vivid primary colors she had. Choosing a large octagon block
interspersed with small diamonds, and making her floral centers in the
popcorn stitch, Leslie found the variation in stitch and design she loves.

SIZE
About 80″ square

MATERIALS
Yarn: Knitting worsted, 30 oz. white (color A); 12 oz. each orange (B) and green (C); 4 oz. yellow (D), about 80 oz. assorted colors for octagon background (if using scraps, allow ¾ oz. or about 50 yd. for each octagon)

Crochet hook: Size F (4.00 mm) or size that gives you correct gauge.

GAUGE
Each octagon measures about 8″ across, straight edge to opposite straight edge; each diamond measures about 4″ from point to opposite point.

STITCHES
Ch, sl st, sc, dc, tr, pc (directions given below)

Degree of difficulty: **

DIRECTIONS
Note: To change colors, fasten off old color at end of rnd; make slip knot (beginning loop) on hook with new color to start next rnd. Conceal yarn ends in work.

Octagons
Make 100. Starting at center with D, ch 5. Join with sl st to form ring.

Rnd 1 (wrong side): Work 8 sc in ring; join with sl st to first sc. Fasten off.

Rnd 2 (wrong side): With B, sl st in any sc, ch 3 (counts as first dc), work 4 more dc in same sc, drop lp from hook, insert hook from back to front through top of ch 3, pick up dropped lp on hook and draw through (first popcorn, pc, made), ch 3, * work 5 dc in next sc, drop lp from hook, insert hook back to front in first dc of this dc group and draw dropped lp through (another pc made), ch 3; repeat from * 6 times more (8 pc made); join to top of first pc. Fasten off. Turn piece to work on right side of work for remaining rnds. Pc should bulge out on right side.

Rnd 3: With desired background color, sl st in first ch of any ch-3 lp, ch 3 (counts as first dc), work 4 more dc over same lp, work 5 dc over each remaining lp (40 dc); join to top of ch 3.

Rnd 4: Ch 3, working in back lp only throughout remaining rnds, dc in next dc, * 3 dc in next dc (corner made), dc in next 4 dc; repeat from * 6 times more, work corner, dc in last 2 dc (8 corners made); join.

Rnd 5: Ch 3, dc in each dc around (no inc made); join.

Rnd 6: Ch 3, dc in next 2 dc, * 3 dc in next dc (corner made), dc in next 6 dc; repeat from * around, ending dc in last 3 dc; join.

Rnds 7 and 8: Ch 3, dc around, working 3 dc in center dc at each corner; join. Fasten off.

Rnd 9: With A, sc in back lp of each dc, working 3 sc in center dc at each corner; join. Fasten off.

Diamonds
Make 81.

Rnds 1 and 2: Work same as for octagon, using C for Rnd 2.

Rnd 3: With A, sl st over any ch-3 lp, ch

3 (counts as first dc), work (4 dc, 2 tr) over same lp, * work (2 tr, 5 dc) over next lp, work (5 dc, 2 tr) over next lp; repeat from * twice more, work (2 tr, 5 dc) over last lp; join.

Rnd 4: Working in back lp only, sc in same place as joining, sc in next 6 sts, * 3 sc in next tr (corner made), sc in next 13 sts; repeat from * twice more, 3 sc in next tr, sc in last 6 sts; join. Fasten off.

Assembly

Lay out octagons in 10 rows of 10 octagons each, with top, bottom, and side edges touching, arranging colors as desired. Fill in spaces between octagons with diamonds.

Joining

Working from wrong side, hold pieces right sides together and use A to crochet adjoining sides together as follows: Start at corner and insert hook under horizontal lp (just below top lps) of sc on front piece (see Figure 17), then down under horizontal lp of corresponding sc on back piece, yo and work sc (unworked top lps will form double row of chain st on right side of afghan); continue to sc in this manner across adjoining edges to next corner. Fasten off. Join all octagons in strips of 10. Join diamonds to one side of each of 9 strips, then fit strips together and crochet together all touching sides of octagons and diamonds.

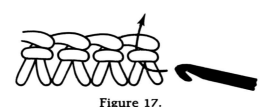

Figure 17.

Flowers and Frames

These pop-up flowers are pretty enough
to be framed—and they are,
by connecting ridges that
surround each charming blossom.

Kim A. Passmore
Curwensville, Pennsylvania

This pattern is the first that Kim has ever designed on her own, and it is a winner! Although she's been crocheting since she was about seven, when her mother taught her, she had always used someone else's pattern.

Kim's quilt is made with baby yarn and a very small hook. The center flower pops up because the center stitches are tightly worked. By joining the units on the right side Kim created raised borders that look like frames for her flowers.

Kim's full-time job is being the best mother she can be to three very active little boys. She and her husband are building their own home, so she doesn't have many spare hours, but when she does, she usually has a crochet hook in her hand. She explains, "It keeps me from eating when I shouldn't."

SIZE

Each square measures 4¼″ across. To make an afghan of the size you desire, see page 165, Designing on Your Own.

MATERIALS

Yarn: Baby yarn; *for each square:* 3 yd. pink (color A), 8 yd. light green (B), 12 yd. white (C), 4 yd. each pale orange (D), yellow (E), blue (F), lavender (G), *plus 7 yd.* desired flower color (A, D, E, F, or G). See page 166 for how to estimate amount of yarn needed for an afghan and also see Note below.

Crochet hook: Size B (2.25 mm) or size that gives you correct gauge.

STITCHES

Ch, sl st, sc, dc, tr cluster st (directions given below)

Degree of difficulty: ***

DIRECTIONS

Note: *Texture:* Original squares were worked very tightly. If you prefer a softer texture, use a larger hook to make a larger square (make practice square to determine amount of extra yarn needed). *Color:* Original afghan is worked with squares in each of 5 flowers colors, with colors joined in diagonal rows.

Work all rnds from right side.

Squares

Starting at center with desired center flower color (A, D, E, F, or G), ch 10. Join with sl st to form ring.

Rnd 1: Ch 3, work 31 dc in ring (32 dc, counting ch 3 as first dc); join to top of ch 3.

Rnd 2: Ch 4, work first tr cluster st (tr-cl) as follows: (Yo twice, insert hook front to back in sp before next dc and bring out in next sp—see Figure 18 A and B; yo and draw up lp, yo and draw through first 2 lps on hook twice) 3 times, yo and draw through all lps on hook (first tr-cl made), * ch 5, work next tr-cl as follows: (Yo twice, insert hook in sp before next dc and bring out in next sp, yo and draw up lp, yo and draw through first 2 lps on hook twice) 4 times, yo and draw through all lps on hook (another tr-cl made); repeat from * around (8 tr-cl made), ch 5; join to top of first tr-cl. Fasten off.

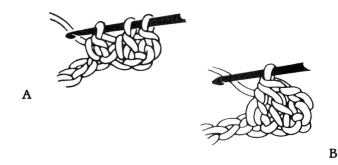

Figure 18.

Rnd 3: Attach B to center of any ch-5 lp, ch 3, 2 dc over same lp, * ch 1, 3 dc over next lp, ch 1, (3 dc, ch 3, 3 dc) over next lp (corner made); repeat from * around, ending with (3 dc, ch 3) over beg lp; join to top of starting ch 3 to complete first corner. Fasten off.

Rnd 4: Attach C to first corner lp, ch 3, 2 dc over same lp, * (ch 1, 3 dc in next ch-1 sp) twice, ch 1, (3 dc, ch 3, 3 dc) over corner lp; repeat from * around, ending with (3 dc, ch 3) over beg lp; join. Fasten off.

Rnd 5: Attach A to any corner lp, * (sc, ch 3, sc) over corner lp, sc in each dc and ch-1 sp to next corner lp; repeat from * around; join to first sc. Fasten off.

Rnd 6: Attach D to any corner lp, * (sc, ch 3, sc) over corner lp, sc in each sc to next corner lp; repeat from * around; join. Fasten off.

Rnds 7 through 10: Repeat Rnd 6 with E, then B, F, and G.

Rnd 11: Attach C to any corner lp, ch 3, dc over same lp, * dc in each sc to next corner lp, (2 dc, ch 3, 2 dc) over corner lp; repeat from * around, ending with 2 dc, ch 3; join to starting ch 3. Fasten off.

Joining
On original afghan, designer used B to sc squares together on right side of work through back lps only of corresponding sts on adjoining edges. This forms a ridge at square edges.

Spring Flowers

**The charm of this design lies in its
unexpected colors, which turned out to be
a good way to use up leftover yarn.**

Geneva Warren
Dora, Alabama

Geneva has been crocheting since she was a teenager and finds it "enjoyable and relaxing." She usually can finish an afghan in a couple of months if she works on it every evening. Her days are full taking care of her family. She and her husband have been married for forty-one years. It seems as if almost always someone among her four sons, two daughters, and thirteen grandchildren needs her attention.

In the splendid design shown here, Geneva has bordered her vibrant spring flowers with a surprising streak of gray that immediately captures the eye.

Geneva is so proud of her design she can't bear to part with it, but she plans to make a duplicate for sale.

SIZE

About 49″ × 67″

MATERIALS

Yarn: Knitting worsted, 3 oz. pale yellow (color A), 18 oz. assorted bright colors for flowers (B), 7 oz. dark green (C), 18 oz. silver gray (D), 22 oz. charcoal heather (E)

Crochet hooks: Sizes I and K (5.50 and 6.50 mm) or sizes that give you correct gauge.

GAUGE

Each square measures 9″ across.

STITCHES

Ch, sl st, sc, dc, pc (directions given below)

Degree of difficulty: **

DIRECTIONS

Note: Work all rnds from right side.

Squares

Make 35. Starting at center with larger hook and color A, ch 4. Join with sl st to form ring.

Rnd 1: Ch 3 (counts as first dc), work 11 more dc in ring; join with sl st to top of ch 3.

Rnd 2: Sc in same place as joining, ch 1, work (sc, ch 1) in each dc around; join to first sc. Fasten off.

Rnd 3: Attach B to any ch-1 sp, ch 3, work 3 dc in same sp, drop lp from hook, insert hook front to back through top of ch 3, pick up dropped lp and pull through (popcorn, pc, made), ch 3, * work 4 dc in next sp, drop lp from hook, insert hook in top of first dc and pull dropped lp through (another pc made), ch 3; repeat from * around; join to top of first pc (12 pc made).

Rnd 4: Sl st in first ch-3 lp, ch 3 and work first pc as before over this first ch-3 lp, ch 2, pc over same loop, ch 2, work (pc, ch 2) twice over each remaining lp around (24 pc); join. Fasten off. Change to smaller hook.

Rnd 5: Attach C to any ch-2 lp, work 3 sc over same lp, work 3 sc over each of next 2 lps, * work 3 dc over next lp, work (3 tr, ch 2, 3 tr) over next lp (corner made), 3 dc over next lp, work sc over each of next 3 lps; repeat from * around, ending with 3 dc over last lp; join. Fasten off.

Rnd 6: Attach D to any corner ch-2 lp, ch 3, work (2 dc, ch 2, 3 dc) over same lp, * work 3 dc in each sp between 3-st groups to next corner, work (3 dc, ch 2, 3 dc) over corner lp; repeat from * around, ending with 3 dc over last lp; join to top of ch 3.

Rnd 7: Ch 3, * work corner in next corner as before, 3 dc in each sp between 3-dc groups to next corner; repeat from * around to last sp, work 2 dc in last sp; join to top of ch 3. Fasten off.

Rnd 8: With E, repeat Rnd 6. Fasten off.

Assembly

Arranging colors as desired, sew squares together through back lps to form panel of 5 squares by 7 squares.

Joining

To sew: Pin together edges to be sewn. Thread needle with matching yarn. Sew edges with whipstitch working through one or both loops (as desired) of corresponding stitches along adjoining edges. Weave yarn ends through corresponding stitches along adjoining edges.

To crochet: With matching yarn, slip stitch or single crochet through corresponding stitches along adjoining edges.

Border

With smaller hook, attach E to any corner lp of afghan.

Rnd 1: Ch 3, (2 dc, ch 2, 3 dc) in same place (first corner worked), * work 3 dc in each sp along edge to next joining, work dc in corner of first square, yo and draw up lp in first corner, yo and draw through first 2 lps on hook, yo and draw up lp in corner of next square, yo and draw through first 2 lps on hook, yo and draw through all lps on hook, work 1 more dc in same place in 2nd square (3-dc group made at joining); repeat from * around, working (3 dc, ch 2, 3 dc) at each corner; join to top of ch 3.

Rnds 2 and 3: Sl st to corner lp, work first corner as before, work 3 dc in each sp around, working (3 dc, ch 2, 3 dc) at each corner; join to top of ch 3. Fasten off at end of Rnd 3.

Delicate Dimensional

This dainty design is worked
in a combination of fine stitches.

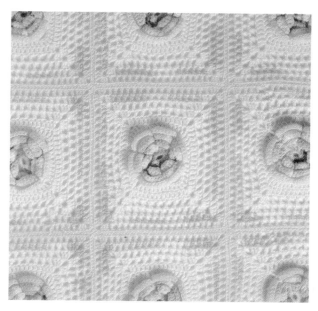

Margaret C. Arnberg
Havelock, North Carolina

Margaret has been crocheting for eighteen years and has made many afghans and scarfs for family and friends. But this is the first time she used a three-dimensional stitch. She chose pastel colors to go with the lacy, delicate filet stitch to create this exquisite square. Since Margaret's three-and-a-half-year-old daughter and two-and-a-half-year-old son keep her occupied during the day, she had to wait until evening to work on this project. It took her three months of evenings to finish.

Like many of the featured craftswomen, Margaret also enjoys other needlework, including crewel and cross-stitch. While Margaret is an accomplished homemaker, her longing for the larger world resulted in her becoming a reservist in the United States Marine Corps. This, she feels is an ideal addition to her life, since "one career offers relief from the other."

SIZE

Each square measures 6¾" across. To make an afghan of the size you desire, see page 165, Designing on Your Own.

MATERIALS

Yarn: Lightweight sport yarn; *for each square:* 23 yd. pastel variegated (color A), 19 yd. yellow (B), 22 yd. white (C). See page 166 for how to estimate amount of yarn needed for an afghan.

Crochet hook: Size E (3.50 mm) or size that gives you correct gauge.

STITCHES

Ch, sl st, sc, dc, tr

Degree of difficulty: ***

DIRECTIONS

Note: Work all rnds from right side.

Square

Starting at center with color A, ch 6. Join with sl st to form ring.

Rnd 1: Ch 3 (counts as first dc), work 11 dc in ring (12 dc, counting ch 3). Do not join, but work around.

Rnd 2: Sc in top of ch 3, (ch 5, sk 1 dc, sc in next dc) 5 times, ch 5; join with sl st to first sc.

Rnd 3 (first petal rnd): Work (sc, 5 tr, sc) over each ch-5 lp; do not join.

Rnd 4: Pushing petals forward out of way and reaching hook behind work, sc in first sc of Rnd 2 (between petal lps), work (ch 6, sc in next sc of Rnd 2) 5 times, ch 6; join with sl st to first sc.

Rnd 5 (2nd petal rnd): Work (sc, 7 tr, sc) over each ch-6 lp. Fasten off.

Rnd 6: Attach B; pushing petals forward out of way, work sc in first sc of Rnd 4, (ch 7, sc in next sc of Rnd 4) 5 times, ch 7; join to first sc.

Rnd 7 (3rd petal rnd): Work (sc, 9 tr, sc) over each ch-7 lp. Fasten off. This completes raised flower.

Rnd 8: For background, attach C; pushing petals forward out of way, work sc in first sc of Rnd 6, (ch 7, sc in next sc of Rnd 6) 5 times, ch 7; join to first sc.

Rnd 9: Ch 3 (counts as first dc), work (dc in each ch of ch-7 lp, dc in next sc) 5 times, dc in each ch of last ch-7 lp; join to top of ch 3 (48 dc, counting ch 3).

Rnd 10: Work (ch 3, dc, ch 3, 2 dc) in same place as joining (first corner made), * dc in next 11 dc, (2 dc, ch 3, 2 dc) in next dc (another corner made); repeat from * twice more, dc in last 11 dc; join to top of ch 3.

Rnd 11: Ch 4, * work (3 dc, ch 3, 3 dc) over corner lp, (ch 1, sk 1 dc, dc in next dc) 7 times, ch 1; repeat from * around, ending last repeat with dc in dc, ch 1, sk last dc; join to 3rd ch of ch 4.

Rnd 12: Ch 4, * dc in center dc of next 3-dc group, ch 1 work (3 dc, ch 3, 3 dc) over corner lp, ch 1, dc in center dc of next 3-dc group, (ch 1, dc in next ch-1 sp) 8 times, ch 1; repeat from * around, ending with dc in last sp, ch 1; join to 3rd ch of ch 4. Fasten off C; attach A.

Rnd 13: Ch 4, * (dc, ch 1) in each sp to next corner, dc in center dc of next 3-dc group, ch 1, (3 dc, ch 3, 3 dc) over corner lp, ch 1, dc in center dc of next 3-dc group, ch 1; repeat from * around, ending with dc in last sp, ch 1; join to 3rd ch of ch 4. Fasten off A; attach B.

Rnd 14: With B, repeat Rnd 13. Fasten off.

Joining

To sew: Pin together edges to be sewn. Thread needle with matching yarn. Sew edges with whipstitch working through one or both loops (as desired) of corresponding stitches along adjoining edges. Weave yarn ends through corresponding stitches along adjoining edges.

To crochet: With matching yarn, slip stitch or single crochet through corresponding stitches along adjoining edges.

Dancing Daisies

This unusual airy square
with a full-blossom floral center
is perfect for small projects.

Ellen Boucher
Reading, Massachusetts

Ellen learned the basic granny square from her sister. Then she started collecting books and teaching herself new stitches and techniques. She is particularly fond of granny squares because they can be made with scraps of yarn and are so portable she can take them anywhere. Less portable, but just as satisfying, is Ellen's other hobby, ceramics.

This dainty floral pattern, with puff stitch center and raised petals, was created especially for the *Woman's Day* contest. It took Ellen about a week to settle on the design and then about two weeks to crochet the squares and sew them together.

Working full time as a cashier at the local supermarket, Ellen knew she wouldn't have enough time to complete an afghan for the contest, so she entered a pillow instead. She intends to make a matching afghan as soon as she has a chance.

SIZE

Each square measures 5½" across. To make an afghan of the size you desire, see page 165, Designing on Your Own.

MATERIALS

Yarn: Knitting worsted; *for each square:* 12½ yd. pink (color A), 22 yd. off-white (B). See page 166 for how to estimate amount of yarn needed for an afghan.

Crochet hook: Size G (4.50 mm) or size that gives correct gauge.

STITCHES

Ch, sl st, sc, hdc, dc, puff st (directions given below)

Degree of difficulty: ***

DIRECTIONS

Note: Work all rnds from right side.

Square

Starting at center with color A, ch 5. Join with sl st to form ring.

Rnd 1: Ch 1, work 8 sc in ring; join to first sc.

Rnd 2: Draw up lp already on hook to ¾" height, (yo and draw up long lp) 4 times in first sc, yo and draw through all lps on hook, ch 1 to fasten (first puff st made), * ch 3, (yo and draw up long lp) 5 times in next sc, yo and draw through all lps on hook, ch 1 (another puff st made); repeat from * around, ch 3; join to top of first puff st.

Rnd 3: Ch 1, * sc in top of puff st, 5 sc over next ch-3 lp; repeat from * around; join to first sc.

Rnd 4: Working in front lp only on this rnd, sk first sc (above puff st), * sc in next sc, hdc in next sc, (dc, ch 1, dc) in next sc, hdc in next sc, sc in next sc (petal made), sl st in next sc (above puff st); repeat from * around, ending with sl st in last sc; join. Fasten off.

Rnd 5: Reaching behind petals to work in back lp only of Rnd 3 sc on this rnd, join B to sc above any puff st, ch 3 (counts as first dc), dc in next sc, * ch 2, sk 3 sc, dc in next 3 sc, ch 5, sk 3 sc, dc in next 3 sc (corner made); repeat from * around, ending with ch 5, sk 3 sc, dc in last sc; join to top of ch-3.

Rnd 6: Sl st to next ch-2 lp, ch 1, sc over same lp, * ch 3, work (3 dc, ch 3, 3 dc) over corner lp, ch 3, sc over next lp; repeat from * around, ending with ch 3; join to first sc.

Rnd 7: Ch 5 (counts as first dc and ch 2), * dc over next lp, ch 2, dc in center dc of next 3-dc group, ch 2, work (2 dc, ch 3, 2 dc) over corner lp, ch 2, dc in center dc of next group, ch 2, dc over next lp, ch 2, dc in next sc, ch 2; repeat from * around, ending with ch 2; join to 3rd ch of ch 5.

Rnd 8: Ch 1, sc in same place as joining, (2 sc over next lp, sc in next dc) 3 times, * sc in next dc, 4 sc over corner lp, sc in next 2 dc, (2 sc over next lp, sc in next dc) 6 times; repeat from * around, ending with 2 sc over last lp; join. Fasten off.

Joining

To sew: Pin together edges to be sewn. Thread needle with matching yarn. Sew edges with whipstitch working through one or both loops (as desired) of corresponding stitches along adjoining edges. Weave yarn ends through corresponding stitches along adjoining edges.

To crochet: With matching yarn, slip stitch or single crochet through corresponding stitches along adjoining edges.

Dogwood Blossoms

Making the yellow centers of these
delicate spring flowers first helped
save time without sacrificing beauty.

Lynn Gibson
Mays Lick, Kentucky

This delightful square with its little white flowers and yellow centers,
its openwork and lacy corners, makes you think of spring. The design
was inspired by Lynn's mom and mother-in-law. Her mom told her
about the contest and predicted she would win, and her mother-in-law
loves dogwood. Since Lynn and her husband farm together, spring has
a special meaning for the whole family.

When Lynn isn't busy with all the chores life on a farm imposes, plus
caring for her stepdaughter and son, she loves to sew and, especially, to
crochet. It can provide instant gratification—this project took Lynn just
two weeks, even though she worked on it only in the evenings. She fig-
ured out how to make the project go faster by making the yellow centers first, then the petals, and then the border. Her lucky mother-in-law
gets to keep the result. Part of Lynn's pleasure is in making things for
family and friends.

SIZE

Each square measures 8″ across. To make an afghan of the size you desire, see page 165, Designing on Your Own.

MATERIALS

Yarn: Knitting worsted; *for each square:* 1½ yd. pale yellow (color A), 4½ yd. white (B), 38 yd. baby blue (C). See page 166 for how to estimate amount of yarn needed for an afghan.

Crochet hook: Size H (5.00 mm) or size that gives you correct gauge.

GAUGE

Each square measures 8″ across.

STITCHES

Ch, sl st, sc, dc, tr, d tr

Degree of difficulty: ***

DIRECTIONS

Note: Work all rnds from right side.

Square

Starting at center with color A, ch 4. Join with sl st to form ring.

Rnd 1: Work 12 sc in ring; join to first sc. Fasten off.

Rnd 2: Join B to any sc, ch 4, tr in same sc, * 2 dc in next sc, (tr, ch 4, sl st) in next sc, (sl st, ch 4, tr) in next sc; repeat from * around, ending (tr, ch 4, sl st) in last sc (4 petals made); join to base of first ch 4. Fasten off.

Rnd 3: Join C to top of starting ch 4 of any petal, ch 3 (counts as first dc), * dc in next tr, ch 2, sk center 2 dc, dc in next tr, dc in top of ch 4, ch 3, d tr (see page 163) in sl st between petals, ch 3 (corner made), dc in first ch 4 of next petal; repeat from *

around, ending with ch 3; join to top of ch 3 to complete corner.

Rnd 4: Ch 3, dc in next dc, * ch 2, dc in next 2 dc, dc in ch-3 sp, ch 3, (dc, ch 2, dc) in corner d tr, ch 3, dc in ch-3 sp, dc in next 2 dc; repeat from * around, ending with dc in last ch-3 sp; join.

Rnd 5: Ch 3, dc in next dc, * ch 2, dc in next 3 dc, dc in next sp, ch 3, 2 dc in next dc, ch 2, 2 dc in next dc, ch 3, dc in next sp, dc in next 3 dc; repeat from * around, ending with dc in last dc; join.

Rnd 6: Ch 3, dc in next dc, * ch 2, dc in next 4 dc, dc in next sp, ch 2, dc in next 2 dc, ch 2, tr in corner sp, ch 2, dc in next 2 dc, ch 2, dc in next sp, dc in next 4 dc; repeat from * around, ending with dc in last 2 dc; join.

Rnd 7: Ch 3, dc in next dc, * ch 2, dc in next 5 dc, dc in next sp, ch 2, dc in next dc, ch 1, dc in next dc, ch 2, (dc, ch 1, dc) in tr, ch 2, dc in next dc, ch 1, dc in next dc, ch 2, dc in next sp, dc in next 5 dc; repeat from * around, ending with dc in last 3 dc; join. Fasten off.

Joining

To sew: Pin together edges to be sewn. Thread needle with matching yarn. Sew edges with whipstitch working through one or both loops (as desired) of corresponding stitches along adjoining edges. Weave yarn ends through corresponding stitches along adjoining edges.

To crochet: With matching yarn, slip stitch or single crochet through corresponding stitches along adjoining edges.

Poinsettias in Snow

**The blazing beauty of the red
poinsettia flower in the snow
is captured in two remarkable squares.**

Nina Kuzenko
Melville, Saskatchewan, Canada

This blooming poinsettia afghan would fill any home with holiday spirit. The pattern combines two squares, a snowflake and a floral. The graceful red petals, yellow centers, and green leaves against the snow-white background produce an invigorating burst of color. And the finished afghan itself is in the shape of a six-pointed snowflake.

This afghan was especially designed as a Christmas present for Nina's daughter, a physician, who doesn't have time to make one for herself.

Nina loves crafts and also does paper tole, macramé, needlepoint, cross-stitch, and crewel embroidery. She has won many awards and prizes for her crochet work in local exhibitions but this is her first national recognition.

Her mother taught her to crochet when she was fourteen and Nina gradually increased her knowledge by reading books and magazines. She became so proficient that for the last fifteen years she has been teaching others the craft at her local community college.

SIZE

About 83″ across (see Note below)

MATERIALS

Yarn: Knitting worsted, 58 oz. white (MC), 1 oz. yellow (color A), 4 oz. red (B), 7 oz. green (C).

Crochet hook: Size G (4.50 mm) or size that gives you correct gauge.

GAUGE

Each hexagon measures 8½″ across from side to side.

STITCHES

Ch, sl st, sc, hdc, dc, tr

Degree of difficulty: ****

DIRECTIONS

Note: Snowflake and poinsettia hexagons are joined to form hexagon-shaped afghan (6-sided and almost circular).

Work all rnds from right side.

Snowflake Hexagons

Make 37. Starting at center with MC, ch 4. Join with sl st to form ring.

Rnd 1: Ch 3, work 17 dc in ring (18 dc, counting ch 3 as first dc); join with sl st in first ch 3.

Rnd 2: Ch 5, (dc in next dc, 2 dc in next dc, dc in next dc, ch 2) 5 times, dc in next dc, 2 dc in next dc; join to 3rd ch of ch 5.

Rnd 3: Ch 5, (2 dc in next dc, dc in next 2 dc, 2 dc in next dc, ch 2) 5 times, 2 dc in next dc, dc in next 2 dc, dc in same place as starting ch; join to 3rd ch of ch 5.

Rnd 4: Ch 5, (2 dc in next dc, dc in next 4 dc, 2 dc in next dc, ch 2) 5 times, 2 dc in next dc, dc in next 4 dc, dc in same place as starting ch; join to 3rd ch of ch 5.

Rnd 5: Ch 6 (counts as first dc and ch-3 lp), * sc over next ch-2 lp, ch 3, dc in next 8 dc, ch 3; repeat from * around, ending with dc in last 7 dc; join to 3rd ch of ch 6.

Rnd 6: Sl st to center of ch-3 lp, sc over same lp, ch 3, sc over next lp, * ch 3, sk 1 dc, dc in next 6 dc, sk last dc, (ch 3, sc over next lp) twice; repeat from * around, ending with dc in 6 dc, sk last dc, ch 3; join to first sc.

Rnd 7: Sl st to center of first lp, sc over same lp, ch 3, sc over next lp, * ch 3, sk 1 dc, dc in 4 dc, sk 1 dc, (ch 3, sc over next lp) 3 times; repeat from * around, ending with sc over last lp, ch 3; join to first sc.

Rnd 8: Sl st to center of first lp, sc over same lp, ch 3, sc over next lp, * ch 3, sk 1 dc, dc in 2 dc, sk 1 dc, (ch 3, sc over next lp) 4 times; repeat from * around, ending with sc over last lp, ch 3; join.

Rnd 9: Ch 3, 3 dc over next lp, dc in sc, * 2 dc over next lp, dc in dc, ch 1, dc in dc, 2 dc over next lp, dc in sc, (3 dc over next lp, dc in sc) 3 times; repeat from * around, ending with 3 dc over last lp; join to top of ch 3. Fasten off.

Poinsettia Hexagons

Make 24. Starting at center with color A, ch 4. Join with sl st to form ring.

Rnd 1: Ch 1, work 12 sc in ring; join with sl st to first sc. Fasten off.

Rnd 2 (petal rnd): Attach B to any sc, ch 1, sc in same sc, * ch 7, sc in 2nd ch from hook, hdc in next ch, dc in next 2 ch, hdc in next ch, sc in last ch (petal made), sc in next sc; repeat from * around, ending with 12th petal; sl st to first sc. Fasten off.

Rnd 3: Attach C to any sc between petals, ch 5, * holding petals forward out of way, dc in next sc between petals, ch 2; repeat from * around; join to 3rd ch of ch 5 (12 ch-2 lps made).

Rnd 4 (leaf rnd): Sc in same place as joining, * ch 8, work sc in 2nd ch from hook, hdc in next ch, dc in next ch, tr in next ch, dc in next ch, hdc in next ch, sc in last ch (leaf made), 2 sc over next ch-2 lp, sc in next dc; repeat from * around, ending with 2 sc over last lp; join to base of first leaf. Fasten off.

Rnd 5: Attach MC to sc just after any leaf, sc in same place, sc in next 2 sc, * holding leaves forward out of way, ch 1, sc in next 3 sc; repeat from * around, ending with ch 1; join to first sc.

Rnd 6 (petal-joining rnd): Ch 1, sc in first 2 sc, * to join petal, drop lp from hook, insert hook front to back through tip of petal, pick up dropped lp and draw through tip of petal, then work sc in next MC sc (petal caught in st), holding leaf forward out of way, 2 sc in ch-1 sp, work sc in next 2 sc; repeat from * around (60 sc); join to first sc.

Rnd 7: Ch 3, holding leaves forward, dc in each sc around; join to top of ch 3.

Rnd 8 (leaf-joining rnd): Ch 3 (counts as first dc), dc in next 4 dc, * to join leaf, drop lp from hook, insert hook front to back through tip of leaf, pick up dropped lp and draw through tip of leaf, work ch 1 (leaf caught in ch 1), dc in next 5 dc; repeat from * around, ending with last leaf caught in ch 1; join to top of ch 3.

Rnd 9: Ch 3, dc in next dc, * (2 tr, ch 2, 2 tr) in next dc (corner made), dc in 2 dc, dc in ch 1, dc in 5 dc, dc in ch 1, dc in 2 dc; repeat from * around, ending with dc in last ch 1 (6 corners made); join to top of ch 3.

Rnd 10: Ch 3, * dc in each st to corner lp, work (2 dc, ch 1, 2 dc) over corner lp; repeat from * around, ending with dc in last st; join. Fasten off.

Assembly

Following Assembly Diagram, Figure 19, for placement, join hexagons, holding right sides of units together and crocheting sc through both lps of corresponding sts of adjoining edges.

Border

Attach MC to any outer corner sp of afghan.

Rnd 1: Ch 4 (counts as first dc and ch-1 sp), work another dc in same place (first outer corner made), then work dc in each dc around, working (dc, ch 1, dc) at each outer corner and dec at each inner corner as follows: (Yo and draw up lp in next st, yo and draw through first 2 lps on hook) twice, yo and draw through all lps on hook. When rnd is completed, join to 3rd ch of ch 4. Fasten off.

Rnds 2 through 5: In same manner work 1 more rnd each with B, then MC, C and MC.

Rnd 6 (scallop rnd): With MC, * (sc, 2 dc) in next dc, sk 2 dc; repeat from * around, working (sc, 2 dc) in each dc and ch at outer corners and skipping 3 dc at inner corners. Fasten off.

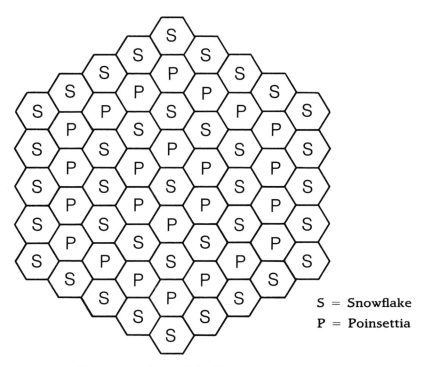

Figure 19. Assembly Diagram

S = Snowflake
P = Poinsettia

Summer Sherbet

Here is a light, airy pattern perfectly
suited for an afghan to ward off
the cool breezes of summer.

Annette Najdek
Bay Shore, New York

These pastel flowers show off their raised petals splendidly against
the light, lacy background. Annette designed the cool, open pattern with
the summer in mind, intending to display the finished afghan on her bed
when the weather turns warm.

Annette has been crocheting since junior high school and learned
from her mother. Lucky friends and relatives are used to getting handmade baby sets and afghans. Annette manages to do her needlework
during the day, between household chores and caring for her ten-year-
old son and twelve-year-old daughter. She has already passed on her
crocheting skills to her daughter, who is just finishing her first scarf.
Annette enjoys reading science fiction when she isn't working at her
other needlecraft hobbies, needlepoint and quilting.

SIZE

Each square measures 11½" across. To make an afghan of the size you desire, see page 165, Designing on Your Own.

MATERIALS

Yarn: Knitting worsted; *for each Square A:* 75 yd. variegated yarn (MC), 35 yd. coordinating solid color (CC); *for each Square B:* 100 yd. variegated yarn (MC), 8 yd. coordinating solid color (CC). See page 166 for how to estimate amount of yarn needed for an afghan.

Crochet hook: Size J (6.00 mm) or size that gives you correct gauge.

STITCHES

Ch, sl st, sc, dc, pc (directions given below)

Degree of difficulty: ***

DIRECTIONS

Note: Work all rnds from right side.

Square A

Starting at center with MC, ch 4. Join with sl st to form ring.

Rnd 1: Ch 5 (counts as first sc and lp), (sc in ring, ch 4) 7 times (8 lps made). Do not join, but work around.

Rnd 2: Work (sc, 4 dc, sc) over each lp around (8 petals made). Do not join.

Rnd 3: * Ch 5, reaching hook behind work, work sc around post below top lps (see page 164) of last sc of next petal; repeat from * around (8 lps made).

Rnd 4: Work (sc, 5 dc, sc) over each lp around.

Rnd 5: * Ch 6, sc around post of last sc of next petal; repeat from * around; join to base of of starting ch 6. Fasten off.

Rnd 6: Attach CC to first ch 6, ch 3, (2 dc, ch 5, 3 dc) over same lp (corner made), * ch 5, sc over next lp, ch 5, work (3 dc, ch 5, 3 dc) over next lp (another corner made); repeat from * around, ending with sc over last lp, ch 5; join to top of ch 3.

Rnd 7: Sl st to corner lp, ch 3, 4 dc over same lp, drop lp from hook, insert hook through top of ch 3 and draw dropped lp through (first popcorn, pc, made), ch 5, work 5 dc over same lp, drop lp from hook, insert hook in first dc of 5-dc group and draw dropped lp through (another pc made), * (ch 5, sc over next lp) to next corner, ch 5, work (pc, ch 5, pc) over corner lp; repeat from * around, ending with sc over last lp, ch 5; join to top of first pc.

Rnds 8 and 9: Repeat Rnd 7. Fasten off at end of Rnd 9.

Rnd 10: Attach MC to any corner lp, ch 3, (2 dc, ch 5, 3 dc) over same lp, * 5 dc over each ch-5 lp to next corner, work (3 dc, ch 5, 3 dc) over corner lp; repeat from * around, ending with 5 dc over last lp; join to top of ch 3.

Rnds 11 and 12: Ch 3, * dc in each dc to next corner lp, work (2 dc, ch 5, 2 dc) over corner lp; repeat from * around, ending dc in last dc; join. Fasten off at end of Rnd 12.

Square B

With CC, work as for Rnds 1 and 2 of Square A. Fasten off CC; attach MC and with MC throughout, complete as for Square A. Fasten off.

Joining

To sew: Pin together edges to be sewn. Thread needle with matching yarn. Sew edges with whipstitch working through one or both loops (as desired) of corresponding stitches along adjoining edges. Weave yarn ends through corresponding stitches along adjoining edges.

To crochet: With matching yarn, slip stitch or single crochet through corresponding stitches along adjoining edges.

Cabbage Rose

These splendid cabbage roses
work up quickly and are the focal point
of an afghan that makes a special baby gift.

Sherry B. Raymer
West Palm Beach, Florida

These lush cabbage roses suggest the fertile Florida terrain. The subtle progression of color, pink to peach to yellow to mint green to blue and lavender, has been carefully choreographed to enhance but not overwhelm the design.

The beauty of the finished product camouflages the fact that this design is quick and easy to execute. In fact, it is based on a design Sherry learned shortly after she first began to crochet, around the age of twelve.

To prove our point, Sherry completed this project in only two weeks, working evenings and a little on weekends. Since Sherry has an eight-year-old son and also teaches preschool, she created a pattern that would make the most of her spare time—and yours. With the time saved, Sherry breeds cockatiel parrots, cooks, bakes, gardens, swims, and bowls.

SIZE

About 30″ × 48″

MATERIALS

Yarn: Knitting worsted, 18 oz. white (MC); 4 oz. each pink (color A), peach (B), yellow (C), green (D), blue (E), lavender (F).

Crochet hook: Size F (4.00 mm) or size that gives you correct gauge.

GAUGE

Each square measures 6″ across.

STITCHES

Ch, sl st, sc, hdc, dc

Degree of difficulty: ***

DIRECTIONS

Note: Work all rnds from right side.

Squares

Make 3 each with center flower worked with A, B, C, D, E, and F. Starting at center with desired flower color, ch 8. Join with sl st to form ring.

Rnd 1: Ch 6 (counts as first dc and ch-3 lp), work (dc in ring, ch 3) 7 times; join with sl st to 3rd ch of starting ch 6 (8 lps made).

Rnd 2 (first petal rnd): Work (sc, hdc, 3 dc, hdc, sc) over each lp; do not join but work around.

Rnd 3: Pushing petals forward out of way and reaching behind work with hook, sl st in joining of Rnd 1, * ch 5, sl st in next dc of Rnd 1 (between petals); repeat from * around; join with sl st to first sl st.

Rnd 4 (2nd petal rnd): Work (sc, hdc, 5 dc, hdc, sc) over each lp; do not join.

Rnd 5: Working behind petals, sl st in joining of Rnd 3, work (ch 7, sl st in next sl st of Rnd 3) around; join with sl st to first sl st.

Rnd 6 (3rd petal rnd): Work (sc, hdc, 7 dc, hdc, sc) over each ch-7 lp; do not join.

Rnd 7: Working behind petals, sl st in joining of Rnd 5, work (ch 9, sl st in next sl st of Rnd 5) around; sl st in first sl st.

Rnd 8 (4th petal rnd): Work (sc, hdc, 9 dc, hdc, sc) over each ch-9 lp. Fasten off. This completes raised flower.

Attach MC to top of center st of any petal.

Rnd 9 (beg background): Ch 3, work (2 dc, ch 2, 3 dc) in same place as joining (first corner made), * ch 6, sc in center st of next petal, ch 6, work (3 dc, ch 2, 3 dc) in center st of next petal (another corner made); repeat from * around, ending last repeat with sc in center st of last petal, ch 6; join to top of ch 3.

Rnd 10: Sl st to first corner lp, work (ch 3, 2 dc, ch 3, 3 dc) in first corner lp, * (ch 3, 3 dc over next ch-6 lp) twice, ch 3, work (3 dc, ch 3, 3 dc) over next corner lp; repeat from * around, ending with 3 dc over last ch-6 lp, ch 3; join to top of ch 3.

Rnd 11: Sl st to first corner lp, * work corner as before, ch 3, (3 dc over next ch-3 lp, ch 3) 3 times; repeat from * around; join to top of starting ch 3. Fasten off.

Assembly

Sew each set of same-color squares together to form 3-square strip, sewing through both lps of corresponding sts along adjoining edges. Sew strips together, starting with A and adding B, then C, D, E, and F strips.

Border

Attach MC to any dc along afghan edge.

Rnd 1: Work sc in each dc and 3 sc over each lp around, working (sc, ch 2, sc) over corner lps; join.

Rnds 2 through 15: Ch 1, sc in each sc around, working (sc, ch 2, sc) over corner lps; join. Fasten off MC at end of Rnd 15.

Rnd 16 (beg rainbow rnds): Attach A to 4th sc after any ch-2 corner lp, ch 3 (counts as first dc), work 2 more dc in same sc, * work (ch 1, sk 3 sc, 3 dc in next sc) to next corner lp (adjusting number of sts skipped as necessary to fit), work (3 dc, ch 1, 3 dc) over corner lp; repeat from * around, ending with 3 dc, ch 1, sk last 3 sc; join to top of ch 3. Fasten off.

Rnd 17: Attach B to any ch-1 sp along side edge, work (ch 3, 2 dc) in same sp, * (ch 1, 3 dc in next sp) to next corner, ch 1, work (3 dc, ch 1, 3 dc) in corner sp; repeat from * around, ending with 3 dc in last sp, ch 1; join to top of ch 3. Fasten off.

Rnds 18 through 21: Repeat Rnd 17 with C, then D, E, and F.

Rnds 22 and 23: Repeat Rnd 17 twice with MC. Do not fasten off.

Rnd 24: Sl st to next ch-1 sp, ch 1, sc in same sp, work (ch 6, sc in next sp) all around, ending ch 6; join to first sc.

Rnd 25: Sl st to center of next lp, ch 1, sc over same lp, work (ch 6, sc over next lp) around, ending ch 6; join to first sc. Fasten off.

Wild Roses

**The crisp green leaves of these
lovely roses are crocheted on
top of a traditional square.**

Mary Dearborn
Reno, Nevada

Here's a splendid easy-to-make granny square by one of our most experienced needleworkers. Mary Dearborn is the mother of four, grandmother of ten, and great-grandmother of five, and many of them have enjoyed the fruits of her crochet hook. Her own mother and grandmother taught her the basic stitches and she learned the rest from books and magazines.

This wild rose design is done on the traditional granny square and the green leaves are attached on top, creating a three-dimensional effect. Mary chose the colors of the wild mountain rose, whose yellow center and pink petals are delicate yet exciting.

Mary usually crochets while listening to the morning and evening news. She has "spent many happy hours crocheting because the end results were rewarding."

SIZE

Each square measures 10″ across. To make an afghan of the size you desire, see page 165, Designing on Your Own.

MATERIALS

Yarn: Knitting worsted; *for each square:* 2½ yd. bright yellow (color A), 9½ yd. bright pink (B), 13 yd. lime green (C), 75 yd. natural (D). See page 166 for how to estimate amounts for afghan.

Crochet hook: Size I (5.50 mm) or size that gives you correct gauge.

STITCHES

Ch, sl st, sc, hdc, dc

Degree of difficulty: ***

DIRECTIONS

Note: Work all rnds from right side.

Square

Starting at center with A, ch 4. Join with sl st to form ring.

Rnd 1: Ch 3 (counts as first dc), 2 dc in ring, ch 3, (3 dc in ring, ch 3) 3 times; join with sl st to top of starting ch 3. Fasten off A; attach B to center of any corner ch-3 lp.

Rnd 2: Ch 6 (counts as dc and ch 3), 3 dc over same lp, * ch 1, (3 dc, ch 3, 3 dc) over next corner lp; repeat from * twice more, ch 1, 2 dc over first corner lp; join to 3rd ch of ch 6.

Rnd 3: Sl st in corner sp, ch 3, (2 dc, ch 3, 3 dc) over first corner lp, * ch 1, 3 dc in next ch-1 sp, ch 1, (3 dc, ch 3, 3 dc) over next corner lp; repeat from * around, ending with 3 dc in last sp, ch 1; join to top of ch 3. Fasten off B.

Leaves: Attach C to any corner lp. * Ch 7, sc in 2nd ch from hook (this is tip of leaf),

hdc in next ch, dc in next 2 ch, hdc in next ch, sc in last ch, sc over same corner lp (leaf made); repeat from * twice more (3 leaves made over lp); ch 3, turn work and sl st to wrong side at base of first leaf (lp made behind base of leaves). Fasten off C. Work 3 leaves over each corner lp in same manner, including ch-3 lp behind work. Attach D to any ch-3 lp behind leaves.

Rnd 4: Holding leaves forward out of way, ch 6, 3 dc over same lp, * ch 1, (3 dc, ch 1) in next 2 ch-1 sp of Rnd 3, work (3 dc, ch 3, 3 dc) over ch-3 lp behind leaves at next corner; repeat from * around, ending with 3 dc in last sp, ch 1, 2 dc over first lp; join to 3rd ch of ch 6.

Rnd 5: Sl st in corner sp, ch 3, (2 dc, ch 3, 3 dc) over first corner lp, * ch 1, (3 dc, ch 1) in each sp to next corner, (3 dc, ch 3, 3 dc) over corner lp; repeat from * around, ending with 3 dc in last sp, ch 1; join to top of ch 3.

Rnd 6 (leaf-joining rnd): Sl st to corner lp, ch 1, sc over corner lp, * insert hook front to back through tip of center leaf, then work sc over corner lp (tip of leaf caught in st), work 1 more sc over same lp, sc in 3 dc, sc in next sp, sc in next 2 dc; catching tip of 3rd leaf in st as before, work sc in next dc, then sc in next sp, sc in 3 dc, sc in next sp; catching tip of first leaf at next corner in st, sc in next dc, then sc in each dc and sp to corner, sc over corner lp; repeat from * around, ending with sc in last 3 dc; join.

Rnd 7: Sl st in next sc where center leaf was joined (corner sc), ch 6, dc in same sc, * (ch 1, sk 1 sc, dc in next sc) to next corner sc, work (dc, ch 3, dc) in corner sc; repeat from * around, ending with ch 1, sk last sc; join to 3rd ch of ch 6.

Rnd 8: Sl st in corner sp, ch 3, (2 dc, ch 3, 3 dc) over first corner sp, * work (ch 1, sk 1 sp, 3 dc in next sp) 5 times, ch 1, sk last sp, (3 dc, ch 3, 3 dc) over corner lp; repeat from * around, ending ch 1, sk last sp; join.

Rnds 9 and 10: Sl st to corner lp, then repeat Rnd 5. Fasten off.

Joining

To sew: Pin together edges to be sewn. Thread needle with matching yarn. Sew edges with whipstitch working through one or both loops (as desired) of corresponding stitches along adjoining edges. Weave yarn ends through corresponding stitches along adjoining edges.

To crochet: With matching yarn, slip stitch or single crochet through corresponding stitches along adjoining edges.

General Directions

- Hooks
- Yarns
- Gauge
- Abbreviations and Terms
- Beginning to Crochet
- Crochet Stitches
- Basic Techniques
- Blocking
- Laundering
- Assembly
- Joining
- Fringes
- Designing on Your Own

HOOKS

Crochet hooks come in a wide range of sizes and lengths and are made of various materials. Steel crochet hooks are generally used for cotton thread and come in sizes 00, the largest, through 14, the smallest. Aluminum and plastic hooks, used for wool, synthetic, and heavy cotton yarns, usually come in sizes B through K, size B being the smallest.

The hook size specified in the directions for each afghan or square is the size most crocheters need to work specified yarn to get the correct gauge. However, you should use the hook size *you* need to get the correct gauge (see Gauge, below).

YARNS

Many of the afghans in this book are made with knitting worsted weight yarn. Sport yarn and baby yarn are used for others. There are variations among brands of the same type of yarn. Baby yarns, for instance, can vary from quite thin to almost as thick as sport yarn. In a few cases, we specified a sturdy-weight baby yarn or indicated the specific yarn used on the original afghan. In general, however, the yarns commonly sold in each weight category should work quite satisfactorily, regardless of brand. Simply use the same weight yarn throughout your afghan.

Traditional granny squares are an inventive way to use up the scraps of yarn that every crocheter seems to accumulate. Although some of the designers purchased yarn especially for their afghans, a number used scraps. Before you begin, check your scraps. Plan to use only those of the weight specified in the directions. Be sure you have an attractive range of colors, filling in needed shades with purchased yarn (for small amounts, check for bargain-priced remnants at your yarn shop). Buy all the yarns you will need at one time, to be sure of having the same dye lot. Slight variations in weight and color can spoil the appearance of your afghan. Whether you buy yarn or use scraps, be sure to use all wool or all synthetic yarns in any one afghan, for ease in care of the completed afghan.

GAUGE

It is important that you crochet to the gauge specified if you wish your squares to fit together smoothly and your afghan to be the correct size. Gauge, in these directions, is usually given as the size of a square (or other unit). Make a practice unit, using the hook and materials specified in the directions. Measure the finished unit to see if it is the correct size.

If your unit does not correspond to the gauge given, experiment with a different-size hook. If you have a smaller unit than specified, use a larger hook; if you have a larger unit than specified, use a smaller hook. Keep changing the hook size until your gauge is the same as that specified.

ABBREVIATIONS AND TERMS

beg	beginning
ch	chain
cl	cluster
dc	double crochet
dec	decrease
d tr	double treble crochet
hdc	half double crochet
inc	increase
lp(s)	loop(s)
MC	main color
rnd(s)	round(s)
sc	single crochet
sk	skip
sl	slip
sl st	slip stitch
sp	space
st(s)	stitch(s)
tog	together
tr	treble crochet
tr tr	treble treble crochet
yo	yarn over

* Repeat the instructions following the asterisk as many times as specified, in addition to the first time.

( ) Repeat the instructions in parentheses as many times as specified. For example, "(Ch 5, sc in next sc) 5 times" means to do all that is specified in the parentheses a total of 5 times.

BEGINNING TO CROCHET

If you are a beginning crocheter, read and practice stitches before beginning an afghan. Experienced crocheters may wish to check afghan instructions for the stitches used and review those stitches. As a general rule, make a practice piece of each new stitch, working until you can do it well and comfortably.

The First Loop (Slip Loop or Slip Knot)

1. Make a loop at the end of the yarn and hold loop in place with thumb and forefinger of left hand. At left is short end of yarn; at right is the long or working yarn (Figure 20A).

Making the loop

20A

2. With right hand, grasp the crochet hook as you would a pencil and put the hook through loop; catch working yarn and draw it through (Figure 20B).

20B

3. Pull short end and working yarn in opposite directions to bring loop close around the end of hook (Figure 20C).

20C

Holding the Thread

1. Measure down working yarn about 4" from loop on hook.

2. At this point, insert yarn between ring finger and little finger of left hand held palm up (Figure 21A).

Holding the thread

3. Weave yarn toward back as shown: down, under little finger and ring finger, over middle finger, and under forefinger toward you (Figure 21B).

4. Grasp hook and loop with thumb and forefinger of left hand.

5. Gently pull working yarn so that it is taut, but not too tight (Figure 21C).

Holding the Hook

1. Hold hook as you would a pencil, but extend middle finger toward tip of hook (Figure 22A).

Holding the hook

2. To begin working, adjust fingers of left hand as in diagram. The middle finger is bent so it can control the tension, while the ring finger and little finger prevent the yarn from moving too freely. As you practice, you will become accustomed to the correct tension. Now you are ready to begin the chain stitch (Figure 22B).

CROCHET STITCHES
Chain Stitch (ch)

1. Pass hook under yarn and catch yarn with hook. This is called yarn over (yo) (Figure 23A).

2. Draw yarn through loop on hook. This makes one chain (Figure 23B).

Chain stitch

3. Repeat steps 1 and 2 until you have as many chain stitches as you need. One loop always remains on hook. Keep thumb and forefinger of your left hand near stitch on which you are working. Practice until chains are uniform.

Slip Stitch (sl st)

Make a foundation chain of 20 stitches for practice piece. Insert hook under 2 top strands of 2nd chain from hook, yarn over. With one motion draw through stitch and loop on hook. Insert hook under 2 top strands of next chain, then yarn over and draw through stitch and loop on hook. Repeat until you have made a slip stitch in each chain (Figure 24).

Slip stitch

24

Note: In all crochet, pick up the 2 top strands of every stitch unless otherwise specified. When only 1 strand is picked up, the effect is different. When instructions say to work "over" a loop, insert hook into the space below the loop, enclosing the loop in the stitch.

Single Crochet (sc)

Make a foundation chain of 20 stitches for practice piece.

1. Insert hook from the front under 2 top strands of 2nd chain from hook (Figure 25A).

Single crochet

25A

2. Yarn over hook (Figure 25B).

25B

3. Draw through stitch. There are 2 loops on hook (Figure 25C).

25C

4. Yarn over (Figure 25D). Draw through 2 loops on hook. One loop remains on hook. One single crochet is completed (Figure 25E).

25D

25E

5. For next single crochet, insert hook under 2 top strands of next stitch. Repeat steps 2, 3, and 4. Make a single crochet in each chain (Figure 25F).

25F

6. At end of row, chain 1 (turning chain) (Figure 25G).

25G

7. Turn work so reverse side is facing you (Figure 25H).

25H

8. Insert hook under 2 top strands of first single crochet. Repeat steps 2, 3, 4, 5, 6, and 7. Continue working single crochet in this manner until work is uniform and you feel familiar with the stitch. On last row, do not make a turning chain. Instead, clip yarn about 3" from work, bring loose end through the one remaining loop on hook, and pull tight. This is called fastening off. You have just completed your practice piece of single crochet (Figure 25I).

25I

Double Crochet (dc)

Make a foundation chain of 20 stitches for practice piece.

1. Yarn over, insert hook under the 2 top strands of 4th chain from hook (Figure 26A).

Double crochet

26A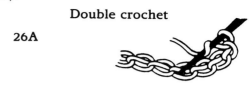

2. Yarn over, draw through stitch. There are now 3 loops on hook.

3. Yarn over (Figure 26B). Draw through 2 loops. Two loops remain on hook.

26B

4. Yarn over again (Figure 26C). Draw through the 2 remaining loops. One loop remains on hook (Figure 26D). One double crochet is now completed.

26C

26D

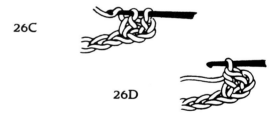

5. For next double crochet, yarn over, insert hook under the 2 top strands of next stitch, and repeat steps 2, 3, and 4. Repeat until you have made a double crochet in each stitch.

6. At end of row, chain 3 and turn work (Figure 26E).

26E

7. On next row, yarn over, skip first double crochet (chain 3 counts as first stitch), insert hook under the 2 top strands of 2nd double crochet. Repeat steps 2, 3, 4, 5, 6, and 7 (Figure 26F).

26F

Note: Work in top chain of turning chain 3 to make last stitch on each row.

8. Continue working double crochet in this manner until work is uniform and you feel familiar with the stitch. On the last row, do not make a turning chain. Instead, clip yarn about 3″ from work, bring loose end through the one remaining loop on hook, and pull tight to fasten off.

Half Double Crochet (hdc)

To make half double crochet, repeat steps 1 and 2 under Double Crochet but insert hook in 3rd chain from hook. At this point there are 3 loops on hook (Figure 27). Then yarn over and draw through all 3 loops at once. Half double crochet is now completed. At end of row, chain 2 to turn.

Half double crochet

27

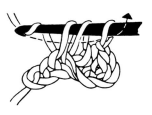

Treble Crochet (tr)

Make a foundation chain of 20 stitches for practice piece.

1. Yarn over twice, insert hook under 2 top strands of 5th chain from hook.

2. Yarn over and draw a loop through the chain. There are now 4 loops on hook.

3. Yarn over again (Figure 28A). Draw through 2 loops on hook (3 loops remain on hook).

Treble crochet

28A

4. Yarn over again (Figure 28B). Draw through 2 loops (2 loops remain on hook).

28B

5. Yarn over again (Figure 28C). Draw through 2 remaining loops (1 loop remains on hook). One treble crochet is now completed. Continue to work a treble crochet in each remaining chain stitch. At end of row, chain 4 to turn. Continue making treble crochet in this manner until you are familiar with the stitch. Finish piece same as other pieces.

28C

Double Treble Crochet (d tr)

To make double treble crochet, yarn over 3 times, then draw up loop in 6th chain from hook (5 loops on hook). Yarn over and draw through first 2 loops on hook (4 loops on hook). Yarn over again and draw through first 2 loops on hook (3 loops on hook). Yarn over again and draw through first 2 loops on hook (2 loops on hook). Yarn over again and draw through both loops on hook (1 loop remains on hook). One double treble crochet is now completed. To turn at end of row, chain 5.

Treble Treble Crochet (tr tr)

To make treble treble crochet, yarn over 4 times, then draw up a loop in 7th chain from hook (6 loops on hook). Yarn over and draw through first 2 loops on hook (5 loops on hook). Work (yarn over and draw through first 2 loops on hook) 4 times more (1 loop remains on hook). One treble treble crochet is now completed. To turn at end of row, chain 6.

BASIC TECHNIQUES

To Turn Work

You will notice that stitches vary in length. Each, therefore, uses a different number of chain stitches to turn at the end of a row. Below is a table showing the number of chain stitches required to make a turn for each stitch.

> Single crochet (sc): ch 1
> Half double crochet (hdc): ch 2
> Double crochet (dc): ch 3
> Treble crochet (tr): ch 4

Double treble crochet (d tr): ch 5
Treble treble crochet (tr tr): ch 6

Note: When it is specified in directions that turning chain is counted as first stitch on new row, skip first stitch of old row before working next stitch after turning chain. Also work into top of turning chain at end of row to maintain correct number of stitches on row.

To Decrease (dec) Single Crochet

1. Work 1 single crochet to point where 2 loops are on hook. Draw up a loop in next stitch (Figure 29A).

Decreasing single crochet

29A

2. Yarn over, draw yarn through 3 loops at one time (Figure 29B). One decrease made.

29B

To Decrease (dec) Double Crochet

1. Work 1 double crochet to point where last 2 loops are on hook. Begin another double crochet in next stitch (4 loops on hook) (Figure 30A).

Decreasing double crochet

30A

2. Yarn over, draw through 2 loops (Figure 30B).

30B

3. Yarn over, draw through 3 loops (Figure 30C). One decrease made.

30C

To Increase (inc)

When directions call for an increase, work 2 stitches in one stitch. This forms one extra stitch.

Slip Stitch for Joining

When directions say "join," always use a slip stitch.

1. Insert hook through the 2 top strands of stitch (Figure 31A).

Slip stitch for joining

31A

2. Yarn over and with one motion draw through stitch and loop on hook (Figure 31B).

Slip stitches are used to join starting chain to form a ring (as shown) or to join last stitch of a round (circular row) to the first stitch.

31B

Working Around the Post

The post or bar is the vertical or upright portion of a stitch. When directions say to make a stitch around the post or bar of a stitch in a previous row, insert the hook around the post from right to left instead of in the top of the stitch (Figure 32).

Working around the post

32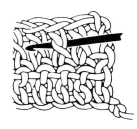

To Change Colors

At the end of round, fasten off old color. You can simply tie on new color or, if you wish to work as many of the designers did, make a slip knot (see page 158) on hook and work slip stitch to attach yarn where specified. (If next round is to be worked in back loop only of stitches, work attaching slip stitch in back loop only of stitch as well.)

To Conceal Yarn Ends in Work

Where possible, hold end of yarn along top

edge of work and crochet stitches over it, concealing it within stitches as you go. Where ends cannot be worked over, weave into wrong side of completed work with crochet hook or with end threaded in yarn needle.

BLOCKING

If an afghan is made up of several pieces, block them before joining them together. If you have laundered your work, block it while it is still damp. If work has not been laundered, dampen it by rolling it up in large damp towel overnight. Place dampened work on a flat padded surface. Gently pat it to the desired measurements; pin to surface, using rustproof pins. Let units dry thoroughly before unpinning.

Note: Do not use an iron for blocking, especially on synthetic yarns, which can melt.

LAUNDERING

If your work has become soiled, wash it by hand before blocking. Launder in cold-water soap or mild soap and lukewarm water. Squeeze but do not wring the piece. Rinse in lukewarm water several times until soap is thoroughly removed. Roll in a bath towel to absorb some of the moisture.

ASSEMBLY

Careful finishing can make or break your afghan, so take time to work neatly.

Follow assembly diagram for placement or lay out pieces as desired in a pleasing arrangement, balancing colors throughout afghan. To keep pieces in order until joined, stack squares in order by row. Pull a length of scrap yarn (threaded on yarn needle), through the stack to tie units together; label each stack with the row number.

JOINING

Many directions specify how the individual designers joined units for the whole afghans. When you join pieces, be sure to match edges stitch by stitch.

Sewing: Pin together edges to be sewn. Thread needle with matching yarn. Sew edges with whipstitch working through one or both loops (as desired) of corresponding stitches along adjoining edges. Weave yarn ends through solid part of crochet.

Crocheting: With matching yarn, slip stitch or single crochet through corresponding stitches along adjoining edges.

FRINGES

Cut yarn strands and fold strands in half. Insert crochet hook through edge of afghan from wrong side and catch strands at fold. Draw loop through. With hook, draw strand ends through loop. Pull ends to tighten knot. When all fringes are completed along edge of afghan, trim ends to an even length.

DESIGNING ON YOUR OWN

You can make many different projects using granny squares: pillows, sweaters, scarves, tote bags, rugs, and placemats as well as afghans and bedspreads. Use the single square designs, or the units from complete afghan designs, to create your own designs. The following techniques will help you plan and make your own afghan or other project.

Choose the design: Select the square you wish to crochet and the yarn you wish to use. The yarns suggested in the individual directions are those used by the designer. Many of the designs can be worked attractively in other yarns—from fine yarns or threads to thick rug yarns—but you must adjust hook size to accommodate your yarn. Work up a sample unit to be sure you like the effect before purchasing materials for an entire project.

Decide on the approximate size of afghan you wish to make (for instance, 36″ × 42″ is a good baby afghan size, 48″ × 60″ is a good lap robe size; larger sizes are good for bed covers). Allowing for border, if desired, *determine the number of squares needed* to make the size afghan you wish. For instance, using 6″ squares for a baby afghan, you could make an afghan of 6 rows with 7 squares each (42 squares in all) with no border added, or a panel of 5 rows with 6 squares each (30 squares in all) with a 3″ border added all around—either measures 36″ × 42″ when finished.

How to estimate amount of yarn needed: The approximate amount of yarn needed in each color to make one square as shown is given under "Yarn." The amount is given in yards to allow you to use scraps and to figure more closely the amount of yarn for your whole project, regardless of size. (If you use a different yarn or hook from those specified, work up a sample square as you wish to make it and determine the amount of yarn needed.)

Check the label of your desired yarn for *yardage.* (If yardage is not given, figure about 150 yards for 1 ounce of baby yarn, 200 yards for 2 ounces of sport yarn, or 220 yards for a 3½-ounce skein of knitting worsted weight yarn.)

Figure amount of yarn needed for *each color* as follows:

  1. Yardage for 1 square _____
  2. Number of squares to be made _____

  3. Multiply step 1 by step 2 (This is total yardage needed for squares.) _____
  4. Divide step 3 by yardage of yarn you wish to use. (This gives you number of skeins needed for squares; be sure to count any leftover fraction as a full skein.) _____
  5. Any extra needed for joining and working border or trim. (Wide afghan borders may require 2, 3, or more extra skeins.) _____
  6. Add steps 4 and 5. (This is the number of skeins needed for the afghan.) _____
  7. Repeat process for each color.

Work the desired number of units for your afghan. See Assembly, page 165.

To join units: Usually squares are sewn together or crocheted with slip stitch or single crochet. Crocheting produces a ridge and can be worked from either the right or wrong side of the afghan as desired. Designers often join units by working through back loops only of adjoining edge stitches; this leaves front loops free, making an attractive outline around each unit.

To finish afghan edges: Some afghans look fine without any border at all. On others a simple border of single crochet or double crochet rows in one or more colors adds a nice frame to the afghan. Or you can look at the complete afghans in this book to see if one of their borders goes well with your design. If you are an experienced crocheter, you may be able to develop your own unique border, picking up colors and stitches or motifs (such as popcorns, shells, cluster stitches) used within squares. Fringes (see page 165), can be used with or without a border to add a finishing touch.

Index

All of us at Meredith® Press are dedicated to offering you, our customer, the best books we can create. We are particularly concerned that all of the instructions for making the projects are clear and accurate. We welcome your comments and would like to hear any suggestions you may have. Please address your correspondence to Customer Service Department, Meredith® Press, Meredith Corporation, 750 Third Avenue, New York, NY 10017.

For information on how you can have *Better Homes and Gardens* delivered to your door, write to: Mr. Robert Austin, P.O. Box 4536, Des Moines, IA 50336.